Jesus at the Helm

by

Jerry Koch

Empyrion Publishing
Winter Garden, FL

Jesus at the Helm
Copyright © 2014 by Jerry Koch

ISBN: 978-0692257647

Empyrion Publishing
PO Box 784327
Winter Garden, FL
Info@EmpyrionPublishing.com

Unless otherwise noted, all Scripture quotations are from the King James Version of the Bible.

New King James is noted as NKJ
New American Standard is noted as NAS
English Standard Version is noted as ESV
Amplified Version is noted as AMP
The Message is noted as MSG

All rights reserved. No part of this book may be reproduced, stored in a retrieval system, or transmitted in any form or by any means - electronic, mechanical, photocopy, recording, or any other, without permission in writing from the author.

Printed in the United States of America

Acknowledgments

Thank you to my wife, Crystal, and my family who always demonstrated that they believed in me and encouraged me to continue in the writing of this book. To my brothers and sisters in the Lord who greatly encouraged me, as well.

And beyond a shadow of a doubt, the Holy Spirit, who caused me to keep my "sails set" when there seemed to be no wind stirring. He always brought the Wind to get me back underway. When going through storms and at my weakest point, Jesus was with me at the helm. And for all the wonderful course headings that my heavenly Father, my "Daddy," had and has planned out for me!

Table of Contents

Introduction	**1**
Chapter 1	
Holy Spirit Sailing Vessel	**11**
Chapter 2	
Spiritual Sailing	**25**
Chapter 3	
Preparing for the Deep	**39**
Chapter 4	
The Rudder, the Tongue	**57**
Chapter 5	
Your Auto Pilot	**75**
Chapter 6	
Integrity	**93**
Chapter 7	
Your Barometer	**111**
Chapter 8	
Spiritual Doldrums	**129**
Chapter 9	
Winds of Many Doctrines	**149**
Chapter 10	
Setting Your Course	**169**
Chapter 11	
Sailing in our Inheritance	**189**
About the Author	**213**

Introduction

Jesus at the Helm was birthed out of a number of years spent on the ocean, sailing mostly through the Caribbean Islands. I had become disillusioned with the previous years in my Christian walk. I had tried to live what I thought was a godly life, but all I could see was how I kept falling short. For some years I had been involved in a Christian ministry for men coming off addictive substances. Without knowing it, I had been trying to live a life of performance under rules of religion and law, plus my own rules. During those years, my relationship with "religion" [trying to please God], left me feeling more separated from Him. In fact, I began to feel I had committed the unpardonable sin and was unsure if there was any way back to God. I finally gave up!

I then slid back into the familiar drugs, alcohol, and bar scene. However, this time was far worse than what I had already been delivered from years earlier. I was searching for a life of excitement and fun, as an escape from God and my thoughts. I chose to mix a cocktail of drugs and alcohol with the freedom of sailing. It is amazing that I could be so deceived as to run from God trying to solve my problems, rather than running to Him

Introduction

for my answer.

It was some years later before I discovered that I had actually been running from a relationship with religion, not a relationship with God. It had been killing me slowly and I didn't even know it.

After those many years of running, I finally came to the end of myself, feeling suicide was a better answer. Before I could devise a painless plan of how to carry it out, I began to feel God's presence in my life again. I was blown away to even think that God would want anything to do with me after all the years of such a decadent lifestyle. I mistakenly thought that since I had once been in the ministry and left it to go back to drugs, sex, and alcohol, that I was put into a special category awaiting certain judgement. Yet, God was extending His Love to me rather than judgement. I could not figure that one out.

He began to show me how much He loved me and that He had never left me, even though I thought our relationship had been severed. This was some kind of Grace! I could not comprehend it! It took me a long time before I could begin to feel comfortable in His presence. I still dealt with condemnation and shame, wanting to feel worthy enough to come to Him.

It was several more years before I came to a revelation of the Grace Gospel, which really is the only gospel. He began to show me that I could give up the performance mentality, trying to be good enough to serve Him. Rather, I was to let Him do what He wanted to do - just let Him love me. However, I still felt it was my duty to love Him back by working hard to serve Him. But it didn't feel right. Deep down, I knew I wasn't doing well and that I was headed right back in the same direction of the labor and works that caused me to fall away in the beginning.

It took some time to understand that my motives were all wrong. He didn't want my service but He wanted my relationship. I was busy trying to convince Jesus that I was following the commandment of love, therefore I deserved His love. And He was busy showing me that I could forget about trying to deserve anything. No one is good enough to deserve His free gift, except by trusting in Jesus. Trying to deserve His love is exactly what closes our hearts, leaving us feeling disqualified. If I would just receive His love, I could then understand how to give love, effortlessly. Receiving first is how our motives change effortlessly.

The New Testament is a covenant between Jesus and the Father, with Jesus representing us believers. This covenant can never fail and is based on our belief and trust in the finished work of Jesus through the cross and His resurrection, not through any of our actions or self effort. In living out this New Covenant, the Holy Spirit began to give me words of knowledge, relating my

Introduction

sailing experiences to my journey through this Christian life. I began to see myself as His "sailing vessel," propelled on this voyage by His "Wind." Although we all will encounter numerous situations on this journey, He will be there with us to bring us through. He will use the experiences we go through to mature us and prepare us for what we will encounter ahead. Just as sailing vessels in the natural are equipped, we, as spiritual sailing vessels, have also been completely equipped.

The better we understand our journey from God's view, which is the Grace Gospel view, the more we will be able to enjoy the trip, getting to where we're going. I will say many times that our destiny is the journey, not the destination.

I will be sharing sailing experiences in the natural realm and how it parallels our journey as His "spiritual sailing vessels." I believe you will be emboldened and encouraged to fearlessly follow the leading of the Holy Spirit as He guides us into the deep blue waters of His Grace! Through this sailing journey, we'll come to better understand our identity in Christ. I believe this "Grace voyage" with our Captain, Jesus, and the Owner of the "Fleet," our heavenly Father, will bring us back to our First Love!

In the next few paragraphs I will give a thumbnail sketch of four parts of a sailing vessel in the natural realm. This will help you to know how they relate to our spiritual sailing vessel.

First, I would like to point out the "keel" of a vessel [see diagram on page 9]. You can see that the keel is the deepest part of the vessel submerged in the water. The keel contains a huge weight called "ballast" which is normally tons of molded lead in todays sailboats. The ballast keeps the vessel standing upright ["on her foot" in sailing terms], through the blowing winds and storms. The ships of old had tons of rocks piled in the keel. On occasion, they were mixed in with hidden, pirated bars of gold and silver. The keel acts as a fin, deep in the water to keep the vessel tracking forward through the seas and not sliding sideways.

So how does that relate to us as a spiritual sailing vessel? Our "spiritual keel" contains the weighty ballast of the Word of God, which keeps us upright, stable, and tracking forward on course through every circumstance of life, during our voyage.

Second, there is the "rudder" located underwater just aft or behind the keel. The bible likens a rudder to be like the "tongue." On any ship or vessel the rudder is connected to the helm, usually a steering wheel. The person at the wheel is called the "helmsman." The helmsman will steer the course heading given him by the "Navigator." You will read more on this in the chapter called, *The Rudder the Tongue*.

Third, you will see the "mast and rigging." If you

Introduction

have walked through a marina, you have likely seen sailboats with a maze of wire cables coming down from the masts and connected to the deck of the boat. These cables, called "standing rigging," hold the mast in place and is what we attach our sails to. The strength of the "mast" is determined by the "integrity" or strength of those cables. Without rigging lines, wind pressure on the sails can topple a mast, causing the vessel to be "dead in the water." Losing a mast can make us like a bobber on the ocean, no longer a sailing vessel. This is true of a "spiritual sailing vessel" as well.

Without God's "integrity" in our spiritual rigging, our spiritual character, the core of our being, cannot withstand the pressures of life. Haven't we seen ministries topple because the integrity of their ministries were compromised. This could be a major hindrance to your journey and destiny. You will read more about this in the chapter entitled *Integrity*. I think you will be surprised about what is said about integrity there.

Fourth, our "sails" are an amazing part of a vessel. They are attached to the rigging and mast to be hoisted up, ready to catch the invisible power of the wind. Although I understand the mechanics of a sail, the physics behind it is still somewhat of a mystery to me. I know they capture the wind and turn it into energy that propels a sailing vessel through the water with speed and power. The speed and stability of a vessel is directly related to the size of the sails hoisted and the speed of the wind.

Now imagine our sails in the spiritual realm catching the "Spiritual Wind." What wind you say? That would be the "Wind of the Holy Spirit" who gives power to our vessel to propel us across the seas of life and on toward our destinations.

> *The wind blows where it wishes and you hear the sound of it, but do not know where it comes from and where it is going;*
>
> John 3:8, NAS

In the spiritual realm, our prayers, praise, worship, and thanksgiving all operate as "spiritual sails" to capture the Wind of the Holy Spirit and propel us through life's seas. Moving by this Spiritual Wind is our "New and Living Way" of traveling on this journey in the New Kingdom. We will see later that not all winds are from the Holy Spirit.

Now, before we begin, let me introduce you to the Ones responsible for this journey we are about to set sail on:

The Owner of our fleet and the Designer of all the plans for our destiny since the foundations of the earth: Our Abba [Daddy] Father!

Introduction

The One who paid for our voyage with His blood and the Captain of our vessel. He gives course headings to our Navigator, intercedes for us and has defeated the enemy: Jesus Christ.

The One who guides us on our course headings, comforts us in this "New and Living Way" of sailing, helps us at the helm and shows us things to come. Our "Wind Power:" The Holy Spirit.

We are now ready to shove off and embark on this awesome voyage! There is a special Wind awaiting to propel us on to our destiny.

...and bringeth forth the wind out of his treasures.
Jer. 51:16, KJV

Let us pull up anchor, hoist our sails and set our course heading for destinations of treasures, surprises, and the unknown. We will be moving through the "Deep Blue Waters" where we will undoubtedly experience His Grace and His Glory. This is where we will find our true identity and fulfill our destiny!

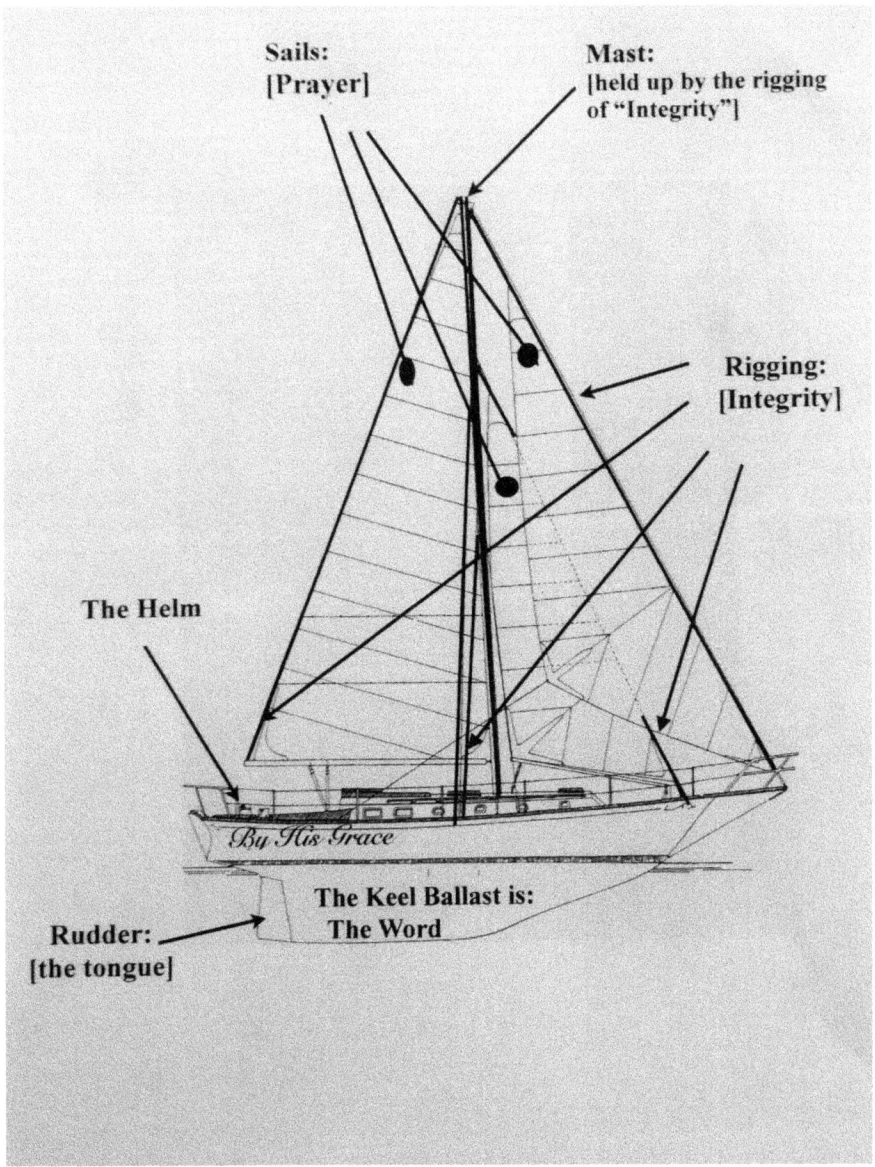

Chapter 1

Holy Spirit Sailing Vessel

[*If you haven't read the introduction, please do so now.*]

Learning to Sail

It was a typical warm, humid, Florida morning and I was standing at the edge of the boatyard where a small canal dead-ends. I was gazing up at my brand new "shippy-looking" sailboat suspended in the air by the launching straps of a crane, having lifted her out of it's cradle. They gently eased her into the canal as she rested noticeably just above the waterline marks. I could't wait to climb aboard and begin my first long distance solo sail. I was beginning this journey on a tight budget with almost no equipment.

Holy Spirit Sailing Vessel

The inside of my boat was just a bare fiberglass hull. No head, no galley, nothing but structural bulkheads to give strength to the hull. My plan would be to finish building the rest of the interior as money became available. It was a job that turned from months into about a year to finish.

I boarded my boat, cranked up the small inboard diesel engine and with all sails hoisted, I motored out of the canal. There were three large bays that I would have to cross, with three bridges to pass under, before I could enter the Gulf of Mexico. One of those bridges would require an "air horn blast" to alert the "bridge tender" to raise up the bridge so I could pass through.

I had just set my air horn on the cockpit deck as I was making my way out of the canal. When I entered the bay, a strong blast of wind hit my sails! Immediately, my boat rolled onto its "chine" [side] and took off, accelerating under sail. Thrilled by the excitement of the moment, I was sailing, but struggling at the helm to get control of my new vessel. Then I remembered the air horn! I turned around just in time to see, as if in slow motion, my air horn being air born. It took a splash into the bay. I looked back over my shoulder towards the shoreline, hoping no one could see what an amateur sailor I really was. Then it hit me, "How am I gonna be able to signal the bridge tender to open up the bridge?" My trip was off to a splashing start!

Jesus at the Helm

Later, as I approached the bridge with no air horn to signal for an opening, I devised a plan to get the bridge tender's attention. I began doing jumping jacks and arm signals on the deck of my boat while yelling, "Open up!" I was now live entertainment for all the cars lined up on the bridge, watching my comical maneuvers in an effort to get the bridge tender's attention. After a lengthy time of my embarrassing charades, he finally opened the bridge.

Within minutes of making my way through the bridge, a small summer squall popped up and quickly blew across the bay. It hit my sails like a freight train. My boat heeled over on her "ear" [side], heading full sail for shore. Trying to bring my boat to a stop, I scrambled to drop sails. Slipping on the wet deck and falling to my knees, I felt great pain!

Finally, regaining control, with all sails covering the deck and looking like a wet shaggy dog, I sat down in the cockpit to rest, thinking to myself, "This sailing definitely takes more savvy than I anticipated! Maybe I should have taken sailing classes after all. Then again, why do things any different than what I've done most of my life anyway?"

By now it was late afternoon and I realized that I had mistakenly and grossly underestimated what I thought would be just a long "day sail." I was now in the second bay and had another large bay to cross before I would enter the Gulf of Mexico. From there it would be another 12 nautical miles south in the Gulf before I would make my inlet. Then I planned to motor my way home to my dock slip. The choice was simple, I would have to drop anchor in Tampa Bay and rest for the night to get a fresh start in the morning. However, there was another problem. My only anchor onboard was very lightweight, borrowed from a small fishing skiff. It wasn't made to hold a sailboat my size. But I decided to give it a try anyway.

I dropped anchor, and gave it plenty of line to grab hold. However, the windage was too much on my boat, causing it to drag the anchor across Tampa Bay. Without the anchor grabbing hold, I had a problem. I would drift towards the shallows as the anchor skipped across the bottom, although it slowed me down a bit. Then, I'd motor upwind, drop anchor and catnap while dragging the anchor toward shore. I repeated this "impressive" nautical maneuver all night. At daybreak, with very little sleep under my belt, still a bit cold and wet from the previous day, I set sail for the Gulf of Mexico.

Finally entering the Gulf, I began on a "port tack" headed offshore. My plan was to make one long tack sailing offshore, then turn and make one long tack back towards the shore. The idea was that two long tacks south would get me to the bay inlet and then easily motor back to the dock slip.

Jesus at the Helm

Inside the cockpit, near my feet, I had a cheap styrofoam cooler with sandwiches, drinks and ice. When I began my first long port tack headed offshore, a gust of wind hit and caught me off guard, again! The boat heeled over on its side as I quickly set my foot out to catch my balance. That's when I heard a loud crunching noise. I knew immediately that I had put my big foot right through the side of the styrofoam cooler. The outcome was inevitable. My drinks, ice, and sandwiches, exposed to the hot Florida summer sun, were doomed. I encouraged myself thinking, "Just one more long tack south and I'll find the bay pass inlet."

However, several hours later, on what I thought to be the last long leg homeward, I was stunned by the appearance of the shoreline. I looked again, and again. Yes, it looked just like the same shoreline I saw as I began my tack offshore. How could this be? To my astonishment I had not sailed 12 nautical miles south. I hadn't even made 5 nautical miles south! In fact, the distance to my destination could have been better measured in *yards* than in nautical miles. It was obvious. I had not yet learned to sail! By this time my sandwiches were mush, the drinks were hot, the ice was melted and I was cookin' in the Florida sun.

Running from God

This was the beginning of many years of my sailing experiences, with no idea where it would lead me. It was also the beginning of taking my "running from God," to a new level. You would think that if I wanted to run from God, I would pick a faster mode of travel than sailing! How deceived can you get?

It wasn't God that I was running from anyway. Rather, it was a relationship I had unknowingly developed with "law and religion." A relationship that was slowly *ebbing life* out of me and so subtly *working death* in me, as it has in so many other lives. I found myself feeling inadequate and condemned when I tried to approach God. I was actually *incarcerated* under "Law" and didn't know it.

The point I want to make is that the loving relationship I had with Jesus was stolen by entering into the realm of rules handed down from laws and religion. I was living proof, no, really "dying proof" of a *ministry of death* and *ministry of condemnation* under the law [2 Cor 3:7-9]. Paul said the law was good when used properly, but it was not made for a "righteous" man [1 Tim.1:8-9]. Trying to be "righteous" by the law is *impossible!* It took Someone perfect to *fulfill the law* for us and Jesus *finished* that work.

Let me "heave to" [pause] here for a moment to give a couple definitions so you understand what I am saying:

Religion is what we think we have to "do" by following rules to get God to bless us or love us.
Law is the rules or commandments we do by our own labor and works to follow after religion.

In reality, salvation is a gift of God, not of works. And our entire journey with God is "Spirit" led, not "works" led.

My hope is that on this journey ahead, you will come to experience a totally new kind of loving relationship that Jesus desires to have with us, no longer based on *our* goodness but based on *His* goodness. You don't have to make the mistakes I made, spending years under the rules of law and traditions of religion. No one can survive a relationship under that kind of yoke.

Our true relationship with God comes through receiving the manifold Grace of God by understanding how He sees us through Jesus and the finished work of the Cross. This is the Grace Gospel that Paul preached. Some things are taught, but I believe this truth is *caught* through revelation by the Holy Spirit.

Even though I tried running from God, unbeknownst to me, He was always there with me. I want to share with you how Jesus used my sailing experiences to parallel them to our Christian journey, as His sailing vessels. As you take this voyage with me, you may feel that you've had similar experiences, even sailing through some of the same waters and wondered how to deal with them. Remember, Jesus can take what may have seemed to be failed voyages and turn them into prosperous, successful voyages. He is our Restorer and will redeem the time. He will show us how to "come about," to get back on course. You may feel like it's too late with too many years of failure. But I'm here to tell you that the years have not passed you by. It's a new day to set sail on a new course to your destiny.

*Do not despise these small beginnings, for the Lord **rejoices** to see the work begin,*
                                   Zechariah 4:10, NLT [emphasis mine]

Salvation under Sail

Our Father rejoices when we set sail on His "course heading" for the deep blue waters of our destiny. Can you imagine with me, as vessels in the "Lord's Fleet of Living Epistles," we are on this sailing journey, propelled by the Wind of the Holy Spirit? Sailing in the Holy Spirit is the new and living way in Jesus. As we begin to understand how to flow in this new way of life, it becomes quite effortless.

Jesus at the Helm

The wind blows where it wishes, and you hear its sound, but you do not know where it comes from or where it goes...

John 3:8, ESV

Salvation is a journey and we are all on this voyage just like any other "mates." You are His precious vessel created to sail across oceans by His Wind. As we step out on this journey together, the Holy Spirit will guide our course. I believe we will learn to feel at home on this journey, just like any other seafaring "Ol' Salts."

At the beginning of each of the following chapters you will read a Word of Knowledge that was given to me by the Lord. The remainder of the chapter will be about how the Holy Spirit is showing us to sail out this particular leg of the journey. Even though all of us may be at different locations on this awesome voyage through life, I believe we will all encounter these same types of situations. I've also included a number of personal experiences, for good or bad, to help give a clearer perspective of this journey with Jesus, our Captain!

As we know Jesus better; his divine power gives us everything we need for living a godly life. He has called us to receive his own glory and goodness!

2 Peter 1:3, NLT

Holy Spirit Sailing Vessel

I have to admit that when I found the answer to the some of the problems I was going through, it was so simple that I just couldn't see it. I couldn't see because I had a veil over my eyes. It was a veil of rules that was covered with sweat – my sweat – from all my labor and work I had been doing in an attempt to please God. I couldn't lift my head up from the weight of the yoke I was carrying. And guess what? I was responsible for that yoke as well as the burden I was carrying. When I said I found the answer, I mean it found me, right in the middle of one of my spiritual voyages headed for the "Port of No Place in Particular." The answer is, well, just keep reading...

We Already Got It

If we understand how our Father sees us through Jesus, it will change how we see ourself and others. Knowing what He has already placed onboard our vessel will change our belief system. We will no longer be on a treasure hunt, trying to find what we already have. Rather, when persuaded that in Christ we have all we need for our journey, we will see things begin to manifest effortlessly in our lives. Peace will come to our hearts as we anchor our security in our identity in Jesus. Let's delight ourselves in Him!

Jesus at the Helm

For that reason, this is NOT a book on how to get *more of* God or *more from* God. My desire is that we will see our Abba Father in a new and living way and become more aware of the gifts and treasures that are placed in each one of us, His treasured children.

This sailing adventure in the spiritual realm may sometimes seem a bit scary as we sail across seas of uncertainty. But our trust is always in the One we have onboard, Jesus. So, with that, we can have a confident expectation of good! How could we expect anything less than *good* from a Father who sent His Son to bring us *life abundant?* His desire is to set us free to be our "New Self," free to sail into the deep blue waters of Grace.

I will never forget when I first recognized the voice of my Father as He spoke to me some years ago. Just three simple words: "God is Fun!" Can you imagine? The first words you hear from your heavenly Father is, "Hey, I'm fun to be around and to hang out with!" Wow! Our God is not a boring God!

Yes, I really needed to hear those words during that specific time in my life. I was battling depression and condemnation. I felt God was holy but He certainly wasn't "fun!" How wrong I was. I can't imagine a more exciting life than this spiritual sailing journey. Trust Him, you haven't seen anything yet!

God puts desires in our hearts and as we recognize those desires and flow with Him, we will be sailing the

Holy Spirit Sailing Vessel

course heading He laid out for us. Let's get in tune with God, focusing on Jesus. We will see the Holy Spirit navigating us to where we need to go. Even if it seems like small beginnings, stay on His course. You will be surprised!

God put sailing in my heart back when I was in third grade. You can't tell me He doesn't know what's ahead in our lives. With the help of a teacher who I still remember very well, she guided me in making the chalk drawing below. It is a drawing of a sailboat, under full sail just off the coast of some island. It's mind boggling just how well God knows us, and what's in our future. Wow!

Jesus at the Helm

Though thy beginning was small, yet thy latter end should greatly increase.

Job 8:7, KJV

Let's set our sails together on this sailing journey to discover who we really are as His special sailing vessels, to experience the abundant life in Jesus, and to know His heart *for us*. We have treasures to discover that He has placed deep inside the innermost part of our vessel, and we will find the "keys" to unlock what we already have while we are on our journey!

Holy Spirit Sailing Vessel

Chapter 2

Spiritual Sailing

You are My chosen vessel. I have created you for my purpose and you are my pleasure and you are my treasure. You are My special vessel set aside for me. I have put you at the helm, but you are not alone. I will always be right there at your shoulder. It is by my Spirit that you will hear my directions. You will hear me speak clearly. Just like the seaman who had a nautical language and would call out "port" or "starboard," you will hear My directions, but in My language. So listen carefully to My Spirit and train yourself to hear My voice. I will not shout but I will speak in a quiet, calm voice. Remember, I am with you and always watching ahead. So, come deeper into my WORD and you will learn My language and understand clearly My words. Learn to enter my peace and rest. It is there you can hear most clearly.

I have many destinations with "ports of call" for you, to many nations and many people. So let not fear have any ground. I am with you. I am training and preparing

Spiritual Sailing

you. But I am putting it in you, my child, to yearn for the deep waters and to desire more. Be prepared to come out into the deep. This is where there is excitement and real life. This is where your destiny will be fulfilled. Let not your heart fear the storms of life nor the waves of circumstances. Neither fear the dark clouds over any uncertain "course headings." I am with you. I have sealed you with my Spirit, "watertight!" Haven't I walked on these oceans and haven't I calmed these seas?

Jesus at the Helm

His Presence

As I've said earlier, I spent a number of years sailing across seas and island hopping as I was "on the run" from God. Even so, deep down I felt He always knew right where I was. The sad news is that I was really running from a wrong and distorted view of God. The good news is that Jesus took those years of running and all the failings in my life and turned them around for my good. Jesus is *never* the author of things that go wrong in our lives, but He is the author of making things work together for our good. Sadly, when we try to run, we always seem to go back to what is familiar. That was me. Little by little I went back to the drug and alcohol scene with the same type of companions I had once left. As a result, I caused a lot of damage to myself and to others.

As I have said earlier, suicide began to look better than keeping on the course I was on. I began to entertain thoughts of how to end it quickly. I had finally come to the end of myself. It was during this time that I began to feel God's presence in my life again. My mind was boggled that He could have a desire for a relationship with me after I had turned my back on Him again and returned to my old life. It was a life of self-indulgence into sex, drugs, and alcohol, trying to bury my thoughts and forget about God. His presence made me realize there's more to this "Grace of God," than what I had ever known!

He is obviously a loving, forgiving God beyond anything I'd ever imagined, but I was still plagued with the relentless feelings of knowing I could never live up to the expectations of a holy God. Yet, after all the things I had done in my past, He was still initiating and pursuing me for a relationship with Him!

During those years of running, feeling lonely and separated from God, I could still at times feel His presence. Little did I know that He was right there at the helm with me, watching over my shoulder. But somehow, I would shake it off and go on. How dumb! It was some years later that He revealed to me that our relationship was never severed, that He had never left me nor forsaken me. Wow! Can you imagine that?

There were times when I sat in the local tavern, a hang out for sailors, and talked with several blokes about the love of Jesus for them. Sometimes, with tears in their eyes, trying to cover their emotions, they would get up and make their exit. Still, I was not able to accept that Jesus could love me too. I thought my ugly self and my wrong stuff was greater than His Grace could handle. Anyway, that's how deceived I was. During all this time of running, He was right there on board with me, even helping me out of tight spots.

Jesus at the Helm

Now, there are probably some who would think, "No way! Jesus doesn't go into bars or places of ill repute." Well, Jesus left the 99 and went after the one that was lost. It is highly unlikely that the one lost was sitting with a bunch of believers talking about the weather. No, the one lost was sitting in the dung like the prodigal son. Jesus is not afraid to wade through the pit to grab up one of His own sheep.

So, my point is that Jesus took my years of running on a sailboat and used them to teach me about my journey with Him. He used my sailing experiences, for good and bad, to teach me how they related to our Kingdom Voyage, not as a parable, but as a parallel. Hence, the title of this chapter, *Spiritual Sailing*. We are His special, treasured sailing vessels in preparation for the voyage ahead according to His plan and purpose for our lives.

A New Freedom

When we receive Christ, we become a *new man*, a new, born again vessel that has never existed before. We are His children, sealed with a new power resident within us, the Holy Spirit. We are no longer propelled through life by our own efforts or strength, but by this "New and Living Way." This new Wind is bringing us to "ports of call," nations and destinations, crossing any seas on His course heading.

Spiritual Sailing

*The wind blows [breathes] where it wills;
and though you hear its sound, yet you neither know where it comes from nor where it is going. So it is with everyone who is born of the Spirit.*

John 3:8, AMP

Remember, this is not a voyage to *prove* anything to God but rather a voyage to *discover* the Love of God, to discover who we are and the treasure we possess. Our destiny is not *in* our destinations but our destiny is *in* our *voyage* on the *way to* our destinations. Just as the Holy Spirit blew His breath of life as a mighty wind through our inner being, He is the breath of wind that navigates us through the seas of life.

God has placed us at the helm of our vessel, but we are not alone. We have a personal Navigator aboard with us and you will hear me speak often of our Navigator. We've been sealed watertight, with the Holy Spirit who gives us directions, guides us, helps us, comforts us through tough seas and stormy nights. He is the one who will encourage us and bring confidence to our hearts of who we are in Christ. This confidence in Jesus brings peace and it persuades our hearts of how faithful He is to never leave us nor forsake us. There will be times when we feel all alone at the helm, but Jesus is right there with us, looking over our shoulder, watching ahead. We need not fear the dark clouds of uncertainty or storms of life. Jesus has already walked on those waters.

Sailing in the *natural* for the most part, has been a way for people to experience and feel the wonderful sense of *freedom*. This is probably the main reason it has attracted so many cruising mates to set sail. When looking at charts of far off islands, a sense of adventure and travel just rises up in you. There is an alluring adrenaline rush of excitement when pointing the bow of your vessel into the spindrift seas, while running down the back side of huge rolling waves, and making your way to new destinations.

What an awesome feeling when you finally make landfall at a Caribbean island! Sailing into those warm breezes, you find yourself entering the kick back, slower paced, island life. You make your way to the leeward of the island to find a protected anchorage. Hidden there from the prevailing winds, you peer over the side of your vessel into the aqua clear waters, searching for a place to drop anchor. On the sandy bottom you see large coral rocks and grassy patches with fish and other sea life moving effortlessly through the water. The clarity of the water suggests that it's not very deep, but surprisingly, the depth finder reveals a reading of 30, 60, or even 100 feet deep. This type of seascape has seized the hearts of many a sailor to anchor them into the cruising, restful life of the "island mentality."

Spiritual Sailing

There is a powerful parallel here. God wants us to see our journey in the spiritual realm as more exciting, more beautiful, more restful than anything in the natural. He gives us freedom from the old "self powered" flesh, to experience a new "Wind powered" Spirit life. It's not about a destination, it's about a "voyage of freedom" with Jesus.

> *It is **for freedom** that Christ has set us free. Stand firm, then, and do not let yourselves be burdened again by a yoke of slavery.*
> Gal. 5:1, NIV [emphasis mine]

There is more to the island mentality than meets the eye. God wants us to enjoy a restful, relaxed voyage, and experience the excitement of new destinations. He will lead us into protected anchorages on the "leeward" side of "blowing problems." We will be able to look into the deep with such clarity in the Spirit that we will now see deeper than ever before. We will be able to see more than just our own life but also into the lives of others around us.

Amazed by the awesome beauty of the "seascape" surrounding us in the spirit realm, we become addicted to a new way of life and a new way of travel. It's here we can enjoy sailing with Him in this new spiritual realm. It's here that we are inspired by new hopes, dreams and desires that have been placed in our hearts. He is wooing us out to the deep blue waters where His Glory is revealed, where we lose our short-sighted focus on the familiar shoreline. We are no longer a slave to fear as we watch land disappear over the horizon. We take a deep breath and the familiar fades away. A yearning for the deep begins to rise up in us. Our focus changes from being on the shoreline to being in Him in the Spiritual Waters of Grace. The presence of Jesus onboard has set us free to enjoy this new journey.

*So if the Son sets you free, you are free **through** and **through**.*

John 8:36, MSG [emphasis mine]

Let's hold fast to that freedom and refuse to let it slip away through the elements of law or religion.

Sailing in the Spiritual realm is a *fluid realm* that at times may seem frightening because we are moving across a spiritual sea where there are no stop signs, no speed limit signs. and no yellow lines. You see, without guidelines or rules, often we feel nervous or insecure. Yet, it's in the spiritual realm that we move and have our being. This is where true life is unveiled and destinies are fulfilled. However, there are some who succumb to the temptation to go back to the familiar where they can still see land and feel a *closeness* to shore.

Let me "heave to" [pause] for a moment here to make a point. I know that, in the natural realm, there has to be rules and laws because not everyone in the world has the Spirit of God, nor do we always operate perfectly by the Spirit of God. Many are sailing blindly through life with their vision obscured by "self" and the "veil of the law," focused only on the natural realm. Many think they need to operate under religious laws or rules, which is really just the world's system of performance. They think this will please God. Jesus has set us free from that burden, so why would we want to go back? Paul warned the Galatians, that turning "astern" [to go back] was an abandonment of their new found freedom.

*Is it not clear to you that to go back to that old rule-keeping, peer-pleasing religion would be an abandonment of everything personal and **free** in my relationship with God? I refuse to do that, to repudiate God's grace.*

Gal. 2:20, MSG [emphasis mine]

God's *freedom* is our inheritance, allowing us to discover our new identity. We're moving out of our natural comfort zone of self effort into the deep blue waters of freedom in the Spirit. In these waters, even the waves have a new sound. It's "Deep calling unto Deep," and by His Spirit there is *liberty*. Here we can come to know our Father more intimately. His desire is to enjoy fellowship with us on this voyage. We are a pleasure to Him and His special treasure. He doesn't just *tolerate* us, He *celebrates* us.

...for it is your Father's good pleasure to give you the kingdom.
Luke 12:32, KJV

His desires become our desires, His good pleasure becomes our good pleasure, His communication becomes our communication, and His will becomes our will.

Through the finished work of the Cross, Jesus purchased our freedom to enjoy that intimate relationship with our Father and we are just sailing in His good pleasure.

For it is God which worketh in you both to will and to do of his good pleasure.
Phil. 2:13, KJV

His Language

We are always in training, learning how to communicate to and behold Jesus. It's an *inner work* He is doing, helping us to hear the wonderful things He is speaking to us. Sailors of old spoke in a different but specific nautical language. They used words peculiar only to sailors that could be clearly understood above the crashing seas on the hull of a vessel. Words, when yelled out during a storm were distinct, not easily confused, such as "port" and "starboard" for left and right. It is in stormy seas and crashing waves that we learn to trust God and in the trusting, we will hear His voice.

> *Trust God from the bottom of your heart; don't try to figure out everything on your own.* **Listen** *for God's* **voice** *in everything you do, everywhere you go; He's the one who will keep you on track* ***[course]***.
> Prov. 3:5-6, MSG [emphasis mine]

We have a Captain that speaks a different language to our hearts. We've been so attuned to hearing language through our natural ears that it's often foreign to us when we begin to hear in the supernatural from our spirit. Jesus said His sheep hear His voice and we do. But sometimes we just don't recognize it. That's why it is so important that we begin to understand how to enter His *rest* and remain in His *peace*. It can be challenging at times to hear or sense His voice through the noise of strife and unrest.

> *My sheep hear my voice,...and they follow me.*
> John 10:27, KJV

Jesus at the Helm

His language and voice becomes clearer as we take time to commune with Him in His Word. The more we *understand* God's *way* of doing things, the more we will *experience* God's *way* of doing things. When waves of problems bring fear and threaten us, we can be confident in knowing that Jesus has already walked on our waves of problems. When the disciples were caught in a storm, He came walking *on* their fear of stormy seas and He does the same for us. When storms rage, winds howl, and seas of circumstances collide with our minds, we will be able to hear clearly, deep down within, a voice speaking to the storm, "Peace, be still."

> *He hushes the storm to a calm and to a gentle whisper, so that the waves of the sea are still.*
> Ps. 107:29, AMP

So, let's relax, set sail and enjoy this new adventure we are called to. It's not easy to be of a fearful heart when we are persuaded of who we have on board. We are now embarking on a voyage of discovering an awesome, unconditional, loving relationship with the Creator of the universe. And after all, it's only for eternity! WOW!

Spiritual Sailing

Chapter 3

Preparing for the Deep

There are many who have yearned for the deep and have said, "It just seems like I am stuck in dry dock and I'll never get a chance to go out to the deep."

Be patient. It is there in dry dock that you'll receive many repairs [changes]. It is there that your rigging can be replaced with My rigging of Integrity. Your mast will not be able to withstand the storms without My rigging.

Then there are some who will say, "All I do is sail up and down this bay and it seems like I am going nowhere and will never see the deep waters." Others will say, "I've had my share of rough waters and I like it better where it is calm and protected. The bay is all I want."

My son, there is preparation ahead, yet. Deep inside of you, in that inner keel of your vessel, you need the heavy ballast of My WORD. This ballast will keep you upright in all conditions. Many see this time of preparation and learning as toilsome, but just know that My Word dwelling deep inside of you will prepare and

Preparing for the Deep

strengthen you for all the seas ahead. It will keep you upright and you will never be put to shame.

This time will also be a time of discovering a "special coating" that I have placed inside of you. It's a covering for you, from stem to stern. This coating provides a special protection from the elements that the "enemy of life" desires to attach to your vessel. This special coating will prevent the enemy from attaching barnacles, seaweed, and slime to your vessel, trying to hinder and slow you down. This coating that I have provided for you, My Anointing, will come from deep within where it abides in you. There is nothing that the enemy can attach to My anointing. He is repelled, struck numb and paralyzed by My Anointing.

You will see how much more easily you can glide through the waters of life and seas of circumstances as you let My Anointing cover you both inside and outside. So, if you're in dry dock, just know that I am doing a preparation in your life for the deep. I'll say it again and again, for the deep!

Dry Dock

During my years of sailing I spent a lot of time in "dry dock" and around boat yards or marinas where sailors hauled their boats out for refitting and repairs. Most sailing mates worked on their boats and helped others out as well. Of course we all had plenty of stories to tell about the cruising trips we had taken. We all had dreams and aspirations about the cruising plans for our future sailing journeys. Some mates had their boats in dry dock for many months with a great deal of repairs. Some, I knew, felt they would never finish preparations on their boat and became discouraged. Feeling like they were stuck in dry dock, they began to think they would never again feel the wind in their sails, or never be able to set sail for the destinations of their dreams.

I believe we have "spiritual dry docks" as well. These are places where we meet together for worship and for the equipping of the saints. It is our place of spiritual refocusing, refitting, and repairs. As born again spiritual vessels, there is training and preparation no matter what our calling. Preparations are really the inner workings of the Holy Spirit, not our self effort training. Self effort is considered dead works which inevitably bring discouragement and can sink our dreams. But if we will turn our focus to Jesus, He will plug the holes.

> *And ye are complete in him, which is the head of all principality and power.*
>
> Col. 2:10, NKJ

In Christ, most of our preparation is discovering what equipment we have been given and learning how to use it. In Him are hidden all the treasures of wisdom and knowledge that we would need for any situation. These are inner treasures that we will discover during our voyage. So when we begin to feel a yearning for the adventures of the Deep Blue Waters, let's trust the Holy Spirit to lead us when we are prepared to step out. He is always at work in us, preparing us for destinations, obstacles, or ports of call that lie ahead. Knowing He is at work in our life gives us rest from feeling stuck in dry dock. Let's flow with Him.

I have to heave to [pause] here to reveal a "caveat." Not just any church, small group, or place of worship is a good place to be for "preparations," even if they use the name of Jesus or Grace. I hope the dry dock where you fellowship is not *dry*, if you catch my meaning. It should be alive with the Grace Gospel. I pray, by the end of this book, you will know when you are in God's boatyard. Trust me, you don't want to end up in a place where you never again feel the wind in your sails and your dreams slowly sink to the bottom of the ocean floor.

> *Then you will have minds confident and at rest, focused on Christ, God's great mystery. All the richest treasures of wisdom and knowledge are embedded in that mystery and nowhere else.*
> Col. 2:2-3, MSG

Love or Fear

Some sailors I knew finished working on their boats and launched them, only to end up sailing around the bay or near the shoreline of the gulf. They were fearful, lacking confidence to set sail for their long planned trips and journey out to the deep. They were more comfortable in the protected waters close to shore. Their focus was on the shoreline rather than on the horizon of the blue waters.

As spiritual vessels, we go through similar experiences. We sometimes encounter fears of getting out in the spiritual blue water where we can only depend on Jesus and not on self. Jesus will help us get past all our fears. He knows that if we will receive His Love, fears are cast out effortlessly without the struggles to get rid of them. Just focus on His Love and fears will leave.

There is no fear in love; but perfect love casts out fear, because fear involves torment. But he who fears has not been made perfect in love.

1 John 4:18, NKJ

A major part of our preparation is learning to *receive* and become conscious of His perfect Love. Focus. Focus!

No Hurry!

On the other hand, in the natural, I have met sailors who did a quick fix at dry dock, dropped their boats into the water and headed for the blue seas. They felt like they had sailed around the bay long enough and even though they were not fully prepared and lacked navigational skills, they headed for deep water anyway. Many of them experienced hard times in stormy seas and within a short time came limping back into port, weatherbeaten and discouraged, their boats in desperate need of repairs. Some were so disillusioned, they decided to give up sailing and put their boats up for sale.

In the spiritual realm, we can short circuit our preparation by setting sail for the deep in an attempt to produce our own ministry by our own power and efforts. That can cause some serious problems. Some have left the ministry, deeply discouraged after hard times and wondering if they were even on the right course to begin with in pursuing their calling. This is why we are to be *led* by the Holy Spirit regarding our calling. If we will put our focus back on Jesus, He will get us back on course. He has given us a Navigator who we can trust.

One very important repair in the natural is the standing rigging or wire cables that holds the mast in place. Unless those lines are of superior quality, they will fatigue and give way, leaving the mast vulnerable to collapsing to the deck (not a pretty site if you have ever seen the results).

In the spiritual, we have lines of "integrity" available for us that have *supernatural* strength. The spiritual rigging in our life is what holds our core parts and values in place. The Lord spoke to me twice about integrity in our lives and that means it's important! So I have a whole chapter devoted to *Integrity*. You may be surprised by what He says about this crucial subject.

The Rock

In the boatyard, I saw about every kind of repair that you could imagine including refurbishing, remodeling and refitting. One major repair, in particular, was the keel and ballast of a boat. It can be a tedious, painstaking job. It is a job that has to be done with expertise. It has to be *right* and *tight*. If not, your boat will never track properly through the water, nor will it stay upright in all kinds of weather. Without heavy ballast in the keel, the wind constantly pushes your vessel onto it's side and rarely will it be upright or sail well on course. Today's vessels have a solid lead weight for ballast as compared to the old "square riggers" that used heavy rocks which sometimes had hidden loot of pirated gold.

Our spiritual vessels need similar preparations in our keel. We need to be filled with the weighty ballast of the Word of God. The Word, deep in the inner keel of our vessel, keeps us upright in any type of sea and never puts us to shame.

Jesus at the Helm

For I am not ashamed of the Gospel of Christ; for it is the power of God unto salvation to everyone that believeth;

Rom. 1:16, KJV

Letting the ballast of the Word find it's place in our deepest core may sometimes seem time-consuming and toilsome, but it is extremely important. Is it toilsome to eat a good meal? Not really! Well, we just need to eat and enjoy the good meal of the Word. Jesus said to feed on His flesh, so let's eat and chew on the Word of God. When we behold Jesus, we see the "Good News" meal. We, however, need to know and understand the difference between "Good News" scriptures and "Bad News" scriptures. Good News is God's Word through a "Grace mentality." Bad News scriptures are read through a "law mentality," which is the leaven of the Pharisees or just plain "religion." The weighty ballast that keeps our vessel upright, has to be "Good News." If we try to use "religion" or Bad News for ballast, it will just take up space like hot air in our keel. We will find no *inner weightiness* in religion to keep us upright and stable. Jesus is the "Word" or "Rock" ballast, that keeps us upright and prepared for any seas ahead.

Scriptures contain the Word of God if we understand them from His view. If we have only mental knowledge and not heart knowledge of the Word, then it is not yet "ballast." That's when the enemy comes quickly to steal the Word before it becomes ballast. He brings storms of circumstances to knock our vessel down, leaving us with condemnation, shame and compromise in our thinking. He uses anything to bring failure and guilt to our lives. It is his way of trying to *spoil* our vessel. However, with the ballast of the Word down deep in our keel, we can get knocked down, but it'll bring us *right back up*. Sailing with a "light- weight keel" [no Word or Bad News] is a recipe for disaster.

Ambassadors

The Gospel of Christ or Good News prepares us to be "commissioned vessels" in Gods fleet. In Noah Webster we see the definition of *commission*:

> "A document authorizing a ship to be employed for specific tasks and responsibilities. Having all equipment in working order and ready for service."

The New Covenant, signed in the blood of Jesus, is the document authorizing His vessels to be commissioned as ambassadors. As I said, we have all the equipment we need in perfect working order, ready for service.

Jesus at the Helm

According as His divine power hath given unto us all things that pertain unto life and godliness, through the knowledge of Him that hath called us to glory and virtue:

2 Peter 1:3, KJV

On this voyage, we're learning the *knowledge* that God has. Through His perspective and His knowledge, we will know how to effortlessly use all that we have been given. It's our destiny! The finished work of the cross, opened up *the way* for us to *know* our heavenly Father, personally! This is where "the Deep" manifests! We are no longer struggling in our performance to see God's blessings, twisting His arm by our works to get His favor. If we will just rest in who we are in Christ, we will receive His blessings through His Grace. This is our new way of thinking and moving in the Kingdom; by His Wind! We are New Covenant vessels in "The Fleet of the Living Epistles" and we fly the banner, "Grace and Truth."

He is the one who has enabled us to represent His new covenant. This is a covenant, not of written laws, but of the Spirit. The old way ends in death; in the new way, the Holy Spirit gives life.

2 Cor. 3:6, NLT

Preparing for the Deep

Anointing

There is another extremely important job that is performed regularly at dry dock. We clean our vessel top to bottom and then apply protective coatings. In particular, a special protective coating of "bottom paint" is applied to the hull, below the waterline, where all the sea growth takes place. This is a protective coating from the growth of barnacles and slimy green moss that attaches itself to the hull of the boat. This moss can easily grow to a foot in length or more in Caribbean waters. Needless to say, it can easily hinder the maneuvering and speed of your vessel. The bottom paint repels, numbs or paralyzes sea growth. It keeps the hull clean, slick, and free from growth so that it can move with ease through the seas.

Now let me bring this into a *spiritual parallel*. Our spiritual coating or bottom paint is the anointing. We are "sealed" with the Holy Spirit, more like we've been vacuum packed, watertight. Our new born again spirit is joined to the Holy Spirit and we are one Spirit with the Lord [1 Cor. 6:17]. The anointing abides in us and manifests from within us. Since the anointing of the Holy Spirit comes from within, we can stop trying to *get* the anointing but rather let what's already abiding in us begin to *manifest*.

Jesus at the Helm

But the anointing which you have received from Him abides in you...

1 John 2:27, NKJ

When we let the anointing flow from inside us, it'll numb and repel the spiritual barnacles of rejection and the slime of condemnation. Anything the enemy tries to put on us will be paralyzed and struck numb by the anointing so that he cannot hinder the destiny of God's vessels. Christ in us, the Anointed One, covers us from stem to stern with His anointing. We need to understand what we have and operate in it so that we flow through the seas of life's struggles with a "New and Living Ease." It does not mean there are no more problems or rough seas ahead. But it does mean that we can sail this journey without the drag of enemy growth on our vessel. He trembles when he sees the anointing covering our vessel, as it slices through the seas, on course for the destinations of God.

Don't Quit

If we see ourselves in dry dock, just know it's a time of preparation for greater things ahead. It's not our home. The Holy Spirit uses this time to reveal who we are in Christ, the treasures within us, and our awesome destiny ahead.

Preparing for the Deep

On this voyage it's not unusual to see times when you just want to *give it up*, to drop the anchor, batten down the hatches, sit in the cockpit under the shade of a bimini top, sipping on a cup of something and watching barnacles grow on the hull of your vessel. However, I have good news for you. There is *never* any shame or condemnation of any sort when going through difficult circumstances. God is never holding anything against us because Jesus already took the blame and the shame on the cross. He knows exactly how we feel and wants us to know that He has walked on those waters and He has our vessel covered, forward and aft!

Though we experience times when we feel like quitting, it may be we have just come to the end of ourselves, and that's a good thing. Often, this is where God can begin to work. We may feel weary or even worn out, but the Holy Spirit will encourage us, comfort us, and lift up of our head. Just don't quit!

God, who got you started in this spiritual adventure, shares with us the life of his Son and our Master Jesus. He will never give up on you. Never forget that.
1 Cor. 1:9, MSG

I have had failed dreams and felt fears about stepping out into the deep. I've been beat up with persecutions and rejection and limped back into harbor opting for calmer waters. I have been disillusioned and left the ministry. I have been in dry dock more times than I care to count and for preparations I don't really understand the "why for." I have stepped out in areas completely unprepared only to come back for relearning and starting over. But I have good news, mate. Jesus never gave up on me and what's more, unbeknownst to me at the time, He never let me quit. He was my strength.

Just Too Good

Just remember, we are victorious because He will always see us through. And the good things ahead will come from a position of *resting* in Him, not *struggling* in our works.

We have some wonderful ports ahead, listed on the "ships itinerary." Yet, we could overlook those destinations if we see them as just too good to be true. The world's kind of reasoning says if it's good, there has to be a *catch*. And religion says, if it's real good, or if it's easy, then it can't be from God. Religion thinks that somehow we have to earn it, to deserve it. Sadly, our unbelief may cause us to pass up a "port of blessing," failing to enter into the harbor to see what God wants to get to us. I've sailed right past blessings in my life because I was on the course heading of "wrong thinking." I almost missed receiving a car from the Lord because it seemed too good to be true. But if we miss it, just repent [meaning to "change your mind"] and refocus on Jesus. He restores. God is good to us, not because we are good, but because He is good!

There are "Harbors of Grace," already on our course heading, waiting for us. Places and times of R & R [rest and refuge]. Failing to enter these harbors to take advantage of that rest, could eventually lead us into the "Bay of Burn Out." Let's trust our Navigator's course plan and His timing. It's always perfect. His course to ports and destinations on this voyage are laid out, planned out, predestined, and waiting for us to discover. Follow Him!

For we are God's masterpiece. He has created us anew in Christ Jesus, so that we can do the good things he planned for us long ago.

Eph. 2:10, NLT

There are plenty of exciting things ahead for us to enter into and see what God is doing. He has given us authority and made us *more than conquerors* to spoil the enemy's schemes and the "Gates of Hell" will not prevail. Our vessel hails the flag, "Favor of God," our source of supply and protection. He has prepared us for the deep blue waters. Look up! With hearts focused on Jesus, we may feel a hand on our shoulder. It's our

Jesus at the Helm

Captain, right there at the helm with us. You will feel His love and rest flowing to you.

> *Look up, and be alert to what is going on around Christ – that's where the action is. See things from his perspective.*
>
> Col. 3:2, MSG

Preparing for the Deep

Chapter 4

The Rudder The Tongue

I am doing a continual preparation in you regarding your tongue. You know, as I have said in my WORD, the tongue is like a rudder that steers a ship. It steers your ship, your vessel. It is very important that your tongue be sensitive to My Word. I have baptized you in the Holy Spirit so that your tongue may be sensitive to Me and to My directions. I have stationed you at the helm of your vessel to be directed through My Word.

It will not be difficult if you will just **trust** *Me and* **rest** *in Me. As you do, you will remain steady on course, not frantically steering from one heading to another, swinging on and off course. Remember, you've not been given a spirit of fear, but of power, love, and* **self-control**. *With this in mind, you will enjoy the ride on the way getting to where you are going. And I will be with you!*

The Rudder, The Tongue

*Don't let the circumstances around you take control of your tongue and put you on a wrong course heading. I will encourage you often of the "precious cargo" you carry, and I have destined you to share it with many others. Yes, there will be those who will refuse to speak My words and will give their tongues over to speak even words of the enemy. They have caused their vessel to steer off course and some have even run aground. I will watch over them son, but to you I say, "Man the helm!" as I direct you by focusing on Me and on My Word. Let the **power** and **fruit of the Spirit** guide your conversation. When you let My Spirit guide your tongue, it will be like an "auto pilot" working within you. You will automatically stay on course, effortlessly following the Wind of the Holy Spirit.*

The Work is Inside

For years I had tried to take control of my tongue and speak the way I thought a godly, holy Christian should speak. I knew I didn't want to run my vessel aground and suffer the consequences. So, I thought, "I've got to work on this tongue thing, to keep my words positive and not speak anything but good, holy, wholesome, positive, Christian words." This was wrong thinking that I had picked up from wrong teaching without knowing it.

Well, unfortunately, the harder I tried the worse it got. Some people with strong will power might see some kind of success with this method, but eventually they'll fail also. Every time something came out of my mouth that was negative I would think, "Well, I've just killed my faith. I've got to start speaking positive." I would mess up time after time. All I could feel was *guilt* and *condemnation*. "Why can't I speak right? Why can't I think right?" I did my best, but it was never good enough. It caused huge problems in my life including falling away from the Lord for close to twenty years.

But it was my religious thinking that caused me to embrace scripture from a law-based mindset. And that was the problem. I couldn't speak right because I didn't believe right and I didn't believe right because I didn't think right. It was some years later when I began to understand the Grace of God. The Lord gave me a Word of Knowledge, which is found at the beginning of this chapter. My desire was to understand that Word from Jesus' perspective of that Word. I was tired of running my vessel aground, trying to live up to what I thought I was supposed to be. That thinking was always born out of my own strength and effort and I knew that it didn't work. It became obvious to me that if my own self effort hadn't worked before I knew Jesus, why should I think it would work after I came to know Him?

As I went over that Word, I saw the answer. It was in the first line and I had missed it for years. In the first line Jesus said He was doing the "work" or "preparation" in me. I failed to focus on the answer, instead I had focused on the problem. It was not up to me to do the work but it was *Jesus* doing the work *in me*. He didn't ask me for my help. He just said that He had stationed me at the helm while He did the work. It's a *continual* work that He is doing. It's not a place that I arrived at, but rather a continuous voyage with ports of call along the way. It's not a final destination but a *destiny of destinations*. In the natural realm, some Christians may travel to the nations and some may not, depending on their calling. But in the spiritual realm, all of us are on a voyage no matter where we are geographically. We carry a special cargo on this voyage, a treasure deep down in our vessel. God has divine appointments that He has arranged for us as we come into ports, bringing our *treasure* to share with others.

Now I could see what preparation He was doing. It was on the *inside* of me and not on the *surface*. He was not interested in surface change that I could produce by myself on the outside. That's just behavior modification. It became evident that I had been suffering from spiritual dyslexia. I was thinking that if I could order my conversation aright on the outside, by my effort, then that would make me right on the inside. The spiritual truth is just the opposite. When the change manifests on the inside, then the words produced and heard on the outside will be the words of LIFE. Jesus said:

For whatever is in your heart determines what you say.

Matt. 12:34, NLT

Righteousness and Grace at the Helm

Yes, the tongue is like a rudder on any ship or any sailing vessel. The direction the rudder is turned will change the direction of the whole vessel. But the direction the rudder is turned is *initiated* at the *helm*. Whatever direction the helmsman steers is the course heading his vessel will take. As the helmsmen, we'll steer according to the heading we *believe* we are to steer.

The Rudder, The Tongue

What I am trying to say here is that we can be deceived. We may think we are steering a good course, but in reality we are letting our tongue [the rudder] take us on a different course, without realizing it.

I remember one time I was installing a new "steering system" in my sail boat, but I inadvertently hooked up the steering cables opposite to what they were supposed to be. You can imagine my surprise, when I turned the steering wheel left, my boat went to the right, and vice versa.

An abundance of wrong teaching will produce wrong thinking that will take our tongue [rudder] off our desired course heading. Hence, wrong thinking produces wrong believing, which puts us on a wrong course heading. Right thinking leads to right believing which puts us on the right course heading. That's why Proverbs says to guard our hearts, for out of it flows the issues of life. There is power in the tongue even though it's a small member of the body. A rudder is a small part of the ship, yet still able to change the direction of a large ship.

> *Likewise, look at the ships; though they are so great and are driven by rough winds, they are steered by a very small rudder wherever the impulse of the helmsman determines.*
>
> James 3:4, AMP

Jesus at the Helm

This verse usually has been ministered in a very negative way. Perhaps because the next verse talks about the tongue setting a forest on fire. But let's see this verse in the light of the Grace Gospel that Paul preached. It will change the way you believe and consequently the way your tongue will steer you. This verse is saying that even though winds of persecution and waves of circumstances come against your vessel, a small thing like the tongue, *when directed by a heart established in Grace, will keep you on course in the face of all negative opposition.* The Message bible says it more directly:

*A small rudder on a huge ship in the hands of a **skilled captain** sets a course in the face of the strongest winds..*
James 3:4, MSG [emphasis mine]

We have a skilled Captain, Jesus, who will teach us by the Holy Spirit how to be skilled at the helm. To do that, we will need to grow up and leave the milk. We will need to understand *righteousness*.

For everyone who partakes only of milk is unskilled in the word of righteousness...
Heb. 5:13, NKJ

What does this have to do with being skillful at the helm? Understanding the "word of righteousness" is probably the greatest piece of knowledge we can have. It will, in turn, make us skillful at the helm and every other area of our lives.

The Word says we are made righteous and sanctified when we are born of God. We are made right with our Father and set apart as His special vessels, not by our works, but by the finished work of the Cross. Our part is to believe and receive the gift of righteousness by faith in Jesus. The disciples asked Jesus what they must do to do the works of God? Jesus said to them, "believe" on Him whom He has sent [John 6:29]. That's it, just *believe*.

> ...*much more they which receive abundance of grace and of the gift of righteousness shall reign in life by one, Jesus Christ.*
>
> Rom. 5:17, KJV

The major part of receiving the gift of righteousness is to understand it's a *gift* and *not earned* by our self efforts or our right doing. True humility is to receive the abundance of grace and the gift of righteousness extended to us as a gift. We need to realize that a gift means it's *free* and we can do nothing to earn it. This is a powerful scripture in having a victorious life, to know we are to reign in life through Jesus, not through works of self effort. We simply believe and receive.

Who is Gonna Control this Tongue?

Most of us were taught, that we were saved by grace, but the rest of the trip depends on us and our own power. That kind of thinking breeds distrust and produces a performance based mentality. That is a voyage of double-mindedness at the helm. Remember, this is not a voyage to see if we can make it by our own efforts. This voyage is really one of discovering how we can *rest* and **let the Holy Spirit do it through us**. He is the One who will make the course heading known to us and He is the One who will get us there. Now the journey becomes fun because the pressure is off!

Since we are talking about the tongue, let's look at the biblical word "confession" meaning to "agree with or to acknowledge the truth" about the Word of God, or in other words, believing and saying about ourselves what Jesus says about us. That is true humility. As we do, faith rises up within us and will keep us on course.

> *...that the sharing of your faith may become effective by the acknowledgment of every good thing which is in you in Christ Jesus.*
>
> Philemon 1:6, NKJ

The Rudder, The Tongue

Using our tongues under the helmsmanship of our Navigator, we will declare all the good things within us in Christ. This verse is really telling us to confess and declare all the treasures that Jesus has placed inside us. That will cause our faith to rise up and become effective. It is declaring our new identity. We are no longer just mouthing confessions to get something, but we are confessing and celebrating what we know we already possess. With our *tongues,* we declare that we are the righteousness of God, that we are the beloved of God, that we have the wisdom of God, that we are prosperous, we are healed by the stripes of Jesus. We have self-control, love, joy, peace, faith, long suffering and all the fruit of the Spirit because it has been placed inside us when we were born of God. The *fruit* of believing is *acknowledging* what we have. Now, our tongue is steering us on the right course.

But you may say, "Now wait a minute, it says in James that no man can tame or control the tongue because it is an unruly evil." The Holy Spirit is saying that **no man** can tame the tongue, that is, the natural or **carnal man** does not possess the power to tame or control the tongue. It takes the power of the Holy Spirit to control the tongue.

[Not in your own strength] for it is God Who is all the while effectually at work in you [energizing and creating in you the power and desire], both to will and to work for His good pleasure and satisfaction and delight.

Phil. 2:13, AMP

Paul told Timothy that he was not given a "spirit of fear, but of power, love and self-control." Paul is saying that the power of self-control comes by the Holy Spirit. Self-control is the fruit of the Spirit. The point I am making is that we need the power of the Holy Spirit to direct and control our tongue. My problem was trying to change the direction of my tongue by my own power, and it never worked.

Tongues of Fire

In James 3, it speaks of the tongue as a fire that can damage a forest of people's lives and our own life. James goes on to describe the carnal tongue as set on fire from hell. Isn't it interesting that in the New Testament we see two different *tongues of fire*? In Acts 2, on the day of Pentecost, the Church is birthed by the Holy Spirit manifesting as *tongues of fire from heaven* that sat upon each of the disciples. They were all filled with the Holy Spirit and spoke in "other tongues" as the Spirit gave

The Rudder, The Tongue

them utterance. The "carnal tongue" of fire that James described destroyed lives. The tongue of fire given by the Holy Spirit saved and added 3,000 lives to the church in one day. This heavenly tongue of fire edified, uplifted and effectively changed the course heading of men for all eternity.

> *For with stammering lips and **another tongue** He will speak to this people, to whom He said, "This is the **rest** with which You may cause the weary to rest," and, "This is the **refreshing**"...*
> Isaiah 28:11-12, NKJ [emphasis mine]

It was God choosing to bring the gift of tongues that birthed the Church. Why not the gift of "ears," or the gift of "noses" or "fingers?" No, He sent the gift of "speaking in tongues" to bring to bear a new power to control a tiny member, the tongue. This would bring rest and refreshing for His sailing vessels. For the children of God, this gift is given to all who will receive it, and it is up to us to exercise the gift we have been given. It produces a change from the inside.

Jesus speaks His desires to our hearts to put us on our course heading through this new and living way of praying in tongues or "in the Spirit." The verse above further says that praying in this manner is the "rest" for the weary and a "refreshing." The word refreshing is found once in the New Testament, in Acts 3:19. It says that times of refreshing come from the presence of the Lord. In the Greek, it means "to cool off" or "recovery of your breath."

So, let's put this all together. Are you hot and thirsty, worn out and weary, tired and out of breath? You've been working too hard at the helm. Pray in the spirit and let the wells of living water flow out from within. Experience the refreshing and rest from the presence of our Lord.

Because we don't really know how to pray as we ought, the Holy Spirit helps us to pray perfectly to God in a tongue that speaks mysteries.

> *For he who speaks in a tongue does not speak to men but to God, for no one understands him; however, in the spirit he speaks mysteries.*
>
> 1 Cor. 14:2, NKJ

Please understand that I am *not* saying that unseemly or ungodly words will never again proceed out of our mouths after receiving this gift. Remember, we are on a voyage and haven't yet arrived. As we "man the helm" and steer the rudder [tongue], let's attend our ear to the Navigator and not to our carnal, un-renewed mind.

The Rudder, The Tongue

We can stop trying to pull ourselves up by our own boot straps and let the Spirit of Grace establish our hearts in the Grace Gospel.

For it is good that the heart be established by grace...
Heb. 13:9, NKJ

Trying to control our tongue by the law or by our own efforts, rules or strength, will only bring frustration and could even run us aground.

I do not frustrate the grace of God; for if righteousness come by the law, then Christ is dead in vain.
Gal. 2:21, KJV

Being established in Grace, however, is the platform from which the Holy Spirit directs our rudder [tongue]. And that, mate, will bring us rest.

The Scuttlebutt

On the Old Square Rigger ships there was a large barrel of water lashed to the gunwale, amidships and a ladle for drinking, hanging off the edge of the barrel. The crew would make their way to the barrel for a break and a quick drink, hopefully to slug down gulps of fresh

Jesus at the Helm

water as they passed the ladle around. But rough seas could easily send splashes of salty sea water over the sides and into the barrel, making it a reservoir of *mixed waters*. As they gathered around this barrel there would be, of course, a lot of sailor stories and jokes being exchanged. Whether truth or fiction, it didn't much matter. This large barrel of water had a name in sailing terms, "the scuttlebutt." Maybe you have heard the expression, "What's the scuttlebutt?" meaning "What's happening?" or more pointedly "What's the latest gossip?" You know, there can be scuttlebutts at the office, scuttlebutts at home, and even scuttlebutts in the Church. As I said earlier, we need to guard our hearts, for out of it proceeds the issues of life. Be careful hanging around the scuttlebutts. You may end up drinking from mixed waters that aren't so fresh. Drinking from those waters could give opportunity for words to cause your rudder [tongue] to get you off course.

Though some tongues just love the taste of gossip, those who follow Jesus have better uses for language than that.

Eph. 5:4, MSG

Through the Holy Spirit we have a new tongue [rudder] that can change our course in the face of all kinds of weather [circumstances]. It is the fiery tongue from *heaven* that we can use to fan the flames and stir up the gifts of life inside us, as Paul spoke to Timothy. Proverbs 18 tells us that *"death* and *life* are in the *power* of the tongue."* We have the power of a Spirit controlled tongue that can set us on the course heading of life. If we listen to our Navigator we will choose life and eat the good fruit of it.

Tree of Life

Let me illustrate from a miracle God performed in the Old Testament as a parallel to the Cross. The Israelites arrived at a place of bitter, poisonous waters, called "Marah" [bitterness]. The Israelites complained to Moses. The Lord showed Moses a "tree" which Moses cast into the waters and the waters became "sweet" and drinkable. The tree represents the Cross of Jesus. When we cast the love of the Cross into the waters of our fountain, it will change it into *sweet, life-giving fresh water*. Let's focus on Jesus and drink from those sweet *living waters*.

*A **wholesome** tongue is a **tree of life**...*
Prov.15:4, KJV [emphasis mine]

Jesus at the Helm

One Hebrew definition for the word "wholesome" is "healing." Imagine a tongue [rudder] that can steer a course of healing in our life and in the lives of others.

James, in his book, warned us that *"no fountain both yields salt water and fresh water."* As we focus on the incredible LOVE of the cross, we will see fountains of fresh living waters *bubble up* from inside us.

...Say only what helps, each word a gift.
Eph. 4:29, MSG

We are not on a voyage looking for treasure, but rather we are on a voyage taking the treasure we have to share it with others.

So, to experience change, we need to focus on the One that brings change and *not* on what needs to be changed. To my surprise, I didn't have a *"rudder-tongue"* problem, but rather a *focus problem*. I believe the more I am occupied with Jesus, the more my Navigator is occupied with the helm, and a certain ease begins to take place at the helm. It kind of feels like there is a supernatural force at the helm keeping me on course. It starts to seem effortless, like it's on auto pilot.

Exactly what is this "auto pilot? Does this mean I just kick back and take my hands off the helm? Is the struggle with my tongue finished? What am I thinking, like I'm on some Caribbean cruise or something? Can I

The Rudder, The Tongue

just relax and rest in the presence of my Captain to enjoy this ride, or am I just being lazy? Wait a minute, mate. Isn't Jesus the author and the finisher of this voyage anyway? Am I supposed to struggle at the helm? Keep reading, the next chapter is titled *Your Auto Pilot*.

Chapter 5

Your Auto Pilot

I am teaching you to be sensitive to the auto pilot I've given you, My Spirit. He will be your guide on this journey because He knows and reads all the intricacies of life ahead of you. He will be like a ship's "navigation station" that reads wind direction and speed, currents and depths, waves and fetch, the weather and pressures, obstacles on the horizon and dangers in the shallows. He will guide you on the best course and the most exciting point of sail, whether it be a "rhumb line" [straight line] or difficult "tacks" [turns].

He is always on board with you and His desire is to help you steer and to give you all course headings. If any adjustments in the course are needed, He will make them, ***in you****. He will show you things to come and will speak those things He hears from the Father.*

I will say it again, you are My Special Vessels carrying My Special Cargo. With hearts of Love, you've been prepared to bring food for the hungry, drink for the

Your Auto Pilot

thirsty, a balm of healing for the sick, a hand for the needy, a hug for the hurting, words of Grace and encouragement for those in despair and salvation to all who will receive it.

This is why the enemy tries to interfere and hinder My Vessels that I have sent to the nations. He will try to send winds of adversity, waves of discouragement, course changes of deception and false readings on your spiritual instruments. One of his most tireless tactics is to bring division among the crew, your mate and your family. But just keep focused on Me and My love for you. As you follow My directions with your whole heart, you will not be deceived.

Jesus at the Helm

The Main Thing

My sailing adventures took me along the coast and intracoastal waters from Maine to Florida, as well to the Bahamas, Central and South America, and the Caribbean. Before I ever set sail I would gather all the information needed for all my destinations. With finances being as they were, I chose my amenities and equipment carefully. I had updated charts, the ship's compass inspected, a good barometer on board, an accurate depth finder, and good binoculars. Two other important pieces of equipment I had on board was a "Satellite Navigation" instrument and a "Wind Vane Auto Pilot" [both of these pieces of equipment are related and I will explain later]. During these years there were only a couple of satellites in space which allowed the read outs on my "Sat. Nav." at 2 ½ hour intervals. That is antiquated by today's standards with numerous satellites giving read outs in micro seconds.

I really treasured my "Wind Vane Auto Pilot." It was able to steer my sailboat by feeling the wind and move the rudder to keep my vessel on course. What a great piece of equipment. Without the auto pilot I would be sitting at the helm, steering my vessel day and night, hardly able to rest. May I add here that most critical mistakes made on sailing journeys that I have heard of and experienced are the result of fatigue. Errors often occur when fatigue sets in, especially when trying to plot navigational headings. Fatigue is an enemy on sailing voyages in the natural and an enemy in our spiritual sailing journeys, as well.

My budget limited the number of amenities I put on board my vessel and compared to many other sailing vessels, mine was sparse. Some would carry water desalinators, ice makers, air-conditioners, etc. A few mates were outfitting their vessels for a comfortable life through the Caribbean and to possibly to sail around the world. They installed all the latest and greatest creature comforts. Yet, many were noticeably lacking more important items, such as navigational equipment and the auto pilot.

My experiences had made me well aware that if I had good navigational equipment, it was a much simpler task to keep my course position accurate and find my way into ports of destination. Once in the port, I could always find necessities, such as fuel, ice and bottled water, etc., but most of all, that long sought-after cheeseburger in paradise. I usually had to search out the local eateries, decorated with a couple wobbling ceiling fans and with all the doors and windows wide open for that famous "island breeze" air conditioning. What more could you ask for? It was like stepping back in time to Bogie and Bacall in "Casablanca!"

Jesus at the Helm

During this time, you could not count on third world countries having their port entry "buoy markers" accurate or even lit up at night. Compared to the US navigational markers and buoys, they were poor, to say the least. Without proper navigational equipment on board, it could be a dangerous task to find your way into certain ports.

What I am saying is that I am all for as many amenities and creature comforts that you can get on board, but not at the expense of the significantly more important navigational equipment. Those comforts lose their importance if you are struggling to make an entry into a port lined with reefs on both sides and you're not sure of your navigational accuracy. There's very little comfort, sitting inside of an A/C cabin, sipping on a drink filled with ice, while the hull of your boat is pounding on a reef that you mistakenly *parked* it on through navigational errors or fatigue. The only thing you'll be thinking about in your panic, as your stomach is all tied up in knots, is "Can I get a 'May Day' in to the U.S. Coast Guard?" Not so likely while offshore of a third world country. My point is this, *make the main thing the main thing!*

Our Auto Pilot

In the spiritual realm, we have the Holy Spirit who is not only our "Navigator," but He is our "Auto Pilot" *if we*

Your Auto Pilot

let Him. Jesus said He would send us the Holy Spirit to *lead* and *guide us,* to be our *comforter and our helper.*

We talked about manning the helm of our spiritual vessel in the previous chapter. But we need a "helper" at the "helm." Therefore, let's make use of what has been given to us. As I've said, fatigue is our enemy. We need to be able to rest on this journey. If we are continually at the helm, occupied with steering our vessel, we will become extremely fatigued and that is when mistakes happen.

In the natural, when I installed the auto pilot on my boat, it made all the difference on my cruising journeys. I was able to take my hands off the helm and rest while the auto pilot did the work of steering my boat. If the wind direction changed, then I made a slight adjustment to the auto pilot and remained on course.

Guiding us is the job of our Navigator since He knows all the intricacies of life that lie ahead. And in the spiritual realm, the Holy Spirit wants to be our *helper*, to be our "auto pilot," to give us *rest* from working at the helm of our vessel and avoid spiritual fatigue.

But the Helper, the Holy Spirit,...the Father will send
John 14:26, NKJ

When I was able to take my hands off the helm and let the auto pilot steer my boat, not only was I able to kick back and *rest*, but I could enjoy the sail. Seeing that my vessel was steering itself effortlessly, I could take time and troll to catch fish. Just a few minutes of trolling with my silver spoon and I'd have a fish from line to landed for my "fresh catch of the day" dinner. What a fresh meal!

This is a great picture of how we should be enjoying our voyage in the spiritual realm. Jesus wants us to relax our minds from laboring at the helm and a constant focus on our destination. He wants us to take time to enjoy His companionship and let Him *fish* with us. Didn't He say He would make us *fishers of men*? How many of us, like Peter, have spent long hours of fishing on our own and caught nothing? Trying to initiate our own ministries, spending long hours fishing only to end up with no fish in the boat. However, just a few minutes of fishing with Jesus brings in net breaking loads! Why not let the Holy Spirit be our auto pilot so we can spend time with Jesus, fishing. Get ready for a boat sinking load, sailing under His banner, *The Grace Gospel*. When the Holy Spirit is our auto pilot we may feel we are not in control as we used to be. Actually, we *are* losing control, no longer depending on "self reliance" but rather on "Jesus reliance."

One time I told the Holy Spirit that I was tired of running my life and I wanted Him to RUN my life. He spoke to me and said, "take the 'I out of 'RUN' and then

Your Auto Pilot

I will RUN your life." I didn't get it at first but then I saw it. When there is the big 'I' in the word 'RUN' it spells, 'RUIN.' He was saying, "Leave yourself, the big 'I,' in the equation and your life will be a 'RUIN.' Get yourself out of the way and I'll 'RUN' your life." It's a burden and tiresome to RUN your own life. Jesus wants to remove the heavy yoke of "works" from our life.

> *Are you tired? Worn out? Burned out on religion? Come to me. Get away with me and you'll recover your life. I'll show you how to take a real rest. Walk **[Sail]** with me and work with me–watch how I do it. Learn the unforced rhythms of grace. I won't lay anything heavy or ill-fitting on you. Keep company with me and you'll learn to live freely and lightly.*
> Matt. 11:28-30, MSG [emphasis mine]

Our Guide

The Holy Spirit is our spiritual "navigation station." In the spirit realm, He knows everything ahead just like we would need to know in the natural – the wind direction, speed, currents, depths, waves, weather pressures, obstacles on the horizon, dangers in the shallows. And He will plot the safest, best, most exciting and fun course heading.

Jesus at the Helm

With the Holy Spirit as our Auto Pilot in the spiritual realm, we'll have time to relax and learn to be ourselves "in Christ," to be who we were *meant* to be. No longer is our focus on "destinations" and our self effort to get us there. He will handle the burden of steering and navigating our course through the circumstances of life. Our Navigator's assignment is to lead and guide us. Can we *rest* in that?

> *...the Spirit of the Truth, He will **take you by the hand** and **guide** you into all the truth there is. He won't draw attention to himself... He will take from me [Jesus] and deliver it to you.*
>
>   John 16:13, MSG [emphasis mine]

The word "guide" here means to "show us the **way**" or the "**journey**." When we allow the Holy Spirit to put His hand to the helm, we find our journey ends up on the right course and we arrive at exactly the right time. He takes what our Skipper, Jesus, says and delivers it to us. As we listen to Him, our course heading becomes clearer.

> *Listen for God's voice in everything you do, everywhere you go; He's the one who will keep you on track **[course]**.*
>
>   Prov. 3:6, MSG [emphasis mine]

Your Auto Pilot

What I am saying is that God has placed His desires in our hearts for destinations and ports of call. We have divine connections ahead, already planned out for us and our Auto Pilot will get us there. I am *not* saying that we are never at the helm any longer. Of course when we are at the helm we are learning to be a skilled helmsman, but it's comforting to know that He is standing with us to help steer and give directions, if we'll let Him. We can rest easy at the helm and let the Holy Spirit put His hands on our hands to help us steer. That's when it feels more like power steering and as if it's almost effortless.

*Likewise the Spirit also **helps** in our weaknesses…*
Rom. 8:26, NKJ [emphasis mine]

Even though this verse refers to prayer, it's also making the point that the Spirit will help us when we are weak. The Greek for "helps" means to "take hold of together against." In other words, the Holy Spirit will take hold of the helm with us, against any problems we are facing. Whether it is storms, fears, doubts, or fatigue. We no longer have to "white knuckle" the helm, trying to steer out of fear and stress, thinking we are all alone.

Jesus at the Helm

Change of Perspective

I'm not saying that we'll never deal with any more problems. In the natural realm, I've been out in the deep, making good headway and suddenly spotted a storm on the horizon. It seemed like it came out of nowhere. There was nothing I could do but go straight *through* it. That storm began to talk to me, trying to get all my attention. The wind was singing through the rigging wires, waves slamming against the hull of the boat and salt spray flying across the deck.

After sailing through a number of storms, my perspective and attitude began to change. Knowing that my sailboat was *made seaworthy,* I could begin to see an excitement in passing through a storm. If I saw a storm on the horizon I would shorten the sails and lash down gear so nothing would get airborne. As the wind hit the sails, my vessel would lunge forward with an exciting acceleration, and I was off and running with the bow of my vessel knifing through the waves, now making headway to my destination at an even faster speed. The rain and wind pelted on a horizontal path across the deck while salt spray flew over my head and I huddled behind the "dodger" [a covering for the cockpit]. The waves would continually wash the deck, but I knew better weather was ahead, on the other side.

Your Auto Pilot

We will experience storms in the spiritual realm as well, but it's not the time to panic and white knuckle the helm, trying to take over the situation in our own strength. Going through spiritual storms in our *own strength*, if we make it through, will only bring us out the other side just as weak, tired and in lack as we were going into the storm. This is the time to get back into *rest* and let the Holy Spirit help us. We may be surprised what happens. Remember, when Jesus is on board, we are going through to the other side!

> *...but I've got my eye on the goal, where God is beckoning us onward – to Jesus. I'm off and running, and I'm not turning back.*
>
> Phil. 3:13, MSG

I believe after we've had a few experiences going through some spiritual storms, our *perspective* and *attitude* will change. This may sound strange, I know, but we may even begin to get excited about some storms because we know they'll just *accelerate* us to our destination, where God has something better on the other side of the storm. We'll begin to feel like eagles soaring over our problems.

What I am saying, is that any way we look at it, we are to *rest* at the helm and let the Holy Spirit help us. Sometimes, with His hands on our hands, we feel almost like we are not even steering. Other times we may hear Him say, "Sit still," and the auto pilot kicks in. When He is at the helm, it's always effortless and He gets us to the right place at the right time, if we'll trust in Him. But if we are continually struggling at the helm, we need to consider *who is **driving** our vessel?*

The Exchange Draws People

We are in the process of exchanging self-confidence, self-reliance and performance for "Jesus reliance" and what He has already performed at the Cross. It is the *great exchange* – our self-esteem for Jesus' esteem, our identity for His identity. It's not just a theological exchange, but a spiritual reality exchange.

God's Word tells us that our new created man has the Father's DNA. As His child we are loved by the Father in just the same way He loves Jesus.

> *But he that is joined unto the Lord is **one** spirit.*
> 1 Cor. 6:17, KJV [emphasis mine]

Now you are one with Jesus, *a joint heir*, a changed heart, taking this Treasure wherever you journey. You carry hugs with words of grace and encouragement to those in despair, words of healing for the sick and hurting, a hand for the needy, food for the hungry, and salvation to thirsty souls.

> *So let's not allow ourselves to get fatigued doing good. At the right time we will harvest a good crop if we don't give up or quit.*
>
> Gal. 6:9, MSG

Let's start to relax on this adventure. God has given us good and perfect gifts to fulfill our journey.

Do you believe that it's *your* job to find *your own way* on this journey? Do you think if you mess up, God will not be there to help you or bless you? But He always will!

The enemy, however, will use any opportunity to bring winds of adversity and waves of discouragement to cause doubt and to get our focus off of Jesus and look elsewhere for an answer. And usually our first choice is *our own efforts*. That, my friend, brings fatigue. The enemy's tactic is to build on fatigue and to bring division on board between us and our mate [spouse]. He is in relentless pursuit to get us off course.

This is why we need the help of the Holy Spirit as our auto pilot. He will make time for us to spend with our mate and our family. Those times when we sense the Holy Spirit prompting us saying, "Follow me, I'm taking you to a place and time of rest to spend with your family." Hey mate, that would be a good time to set sail on His course heading. Otherwise we could find ourself on a destination for the "harbor of desperation." It's quality time spent with our family that brings *life* into relationships and will help us sail around unnecessary storms so we can experience a voyage free of division and strife.

Whose Reflection Do You See?

I remember sailing into some hidden anchorages tucked back into the landscape of Caribbean islands. I was awed by the beautiful, crystal clear waters. I could lean over the side and peer deep down into those calm waters. As I did, I could see my reflection, as in a mirror. It was mesmerizing to gaze into those waters sliding past my vessel.

We need to take time on this journey to gaze into the beautiful, crystal clear, spiritual waters of the Word. As you do, you may see an amazing reflection, a reflection of you. It's the new you. But you look again and you will see it's the reflection of our Lord. Yes, it's Jesus in YOU! You are beholding Him face to face. It's the Glory of the Lord in you! You can see clearer now, like a veil has been removed from your eyes, like someone took a towel and wiped fog off of a mirror. Something has changed and it is in us!

But we all, with unveiled face, beholding as in a mirror the glory of the Lord, are being transformed into the same image from glory to glory, just as by the Spirit of the Lord.

2 Cor. 3:18, NKJ

It is *Christ in us,* a cargo of immeasurable value, as we travel in this "New and Living Way." Yet, amazingly, through His unfathomable love, He counts *us* as *His* treasure! The value of anything is determined by what someone will pay for it. Well, Jesus so treasured us that He gave His life as a ransom to purchase us, to free us from the chains of self-reliance, and to bring a new freedom and liberty found only in our *new re-created self.* That is *His amazing grace!*

Peering further into those crystal clear spiritual waters, it brings some questions to mind. For example, how did this effortless change happen? It hardly felt like *I* did anything, kind of like I've been on auto pilot.

It wasn't our doing, but was our destiny unfolding right before us. It took place from the inside and not from the outside. It was *His* doing.

Now we can simply "shine," letting what's in us, flow out. People are drawn to us because of the light within us. You see, our **identity** *is* our **destiny**!

Jesus at the Helm

> ***Arise, shine****; for thy light is come, and the glory of the Lord is risen upon thee. 2]...but the Lord shall arise upon thee, and His glory shall be seen upon thee.*
>
> Isaiah 60:1-2, KJV [emphasis mine]

Our true identity is *never imparted* through our own efforts. It's only by this new and living way that reveals a true perspective of who we are in Christ. Let's view things from Jesus's perspective.

> *Look up, and be alert to what is going on around Christ – that's where the action is. See things from his perspective.*
>
> Col. 3:2, MSG

This is the time to get in the flow of the *unforced rhythms of grace,* and cease from striving at the helm. Let Him take over and just flow with Him. It's time to surrender, to just say, "Lord, you take over. I'll watch you in action, and see how you do it."

There will still be times when we grab the helm in fear, but we can be confident that Jesus will put His hands on ours to help us steer. He is our intimate friend standing right behind us, to help in time of need. No matter what storms come our way, we can still look to

Your Auto Pilot

Him and see His peace manifest within us, even in the midst of the storm.

It's by His *Grace*, that we're on this sailing journey and it's by His *Grace* that we'll make it home. Welcome to His effortless Grace. This is our destined adventure, *Jesus at the Helm!*

Chapter 6

Integrity

My son, guard your heart with all vigilance from the world's ways and you'll not get entangled again in the world's system. I have been preparing you, a vessel with a tall and sturdy mast, carrying large sails to move you with power and speed across the seas of life. Your mast is to be held in place by the rigging lines of "My Integrity" that I have placed in you. Those who rely on the rigging lines of their "own integrity," produced through their own efforts, will see those rigging lines become loose and weak. Their mast can give way to the storms of life and come crashing to the deck, bringing injury to those on board.

So check yourself and your ways. Is the integrity of your rigging lines your own integrity which you have provided by your own efforts? Or are they lines of integrity that I have provided for you through the Cross? The strength in the rigging lines of My Integrity cannot

Integrity

be broken, as they are unimpaired by the weakness of the flesh. No matter what storms you go through nor how hard the wind blows, your mast, with my "lines of integrity," will remain in place and stable. You will not suffer damage or shipwreck as some have when their self-produced lines of integrity have given way, leaving a broken mast and a vessel in need of repair. Remember, if your rigging lines need any adjusting to take out the slack, it's HOPE that will always keep them taut. Check yourself in every area to discover what has been placed inside you.

Jesus at the Helm

Integrity – Ours or Jesus'?

I hope you can see the picture here. Integrity is represented by the lines or cables that hold the mast of a sailing vessel stable and firmly in place. In sailing terms, these lines are called "standing rigging." If these rigging lines are made of inferior materials, they become loose and the mast can give way or break and topple to the deck. This can cause injury to the crew and damage to the vessel.

In the spiritual, we are the *Vessels of Living Epistles* and need to let the new lines of integrity placed inside of our new man, be our strength. They are "tight and right," and are the *uncompromisingly core strength* of our spiritual mast. Old rigging lines of integrity created from our own efforts and our own rules of performance are impaired, inferior, and compromised. These lines of integrity are produced or initiated through the Law or rules of religion and they, like the flesh, are weak. They become hard, brittle lines that will fatigue and break.

Jesus warned against putting "New Covenant wine" into "Old Covenant wine skins," resulting in the old skins bursting and everything spilling to the ground. Why? It is because Old Covenant wineskins are hard and brittle like the Old Covenant law and commandments that are on stone. The Old Law System cannot be *mixed* with the New Covenant Life that's been placed in our newly created vessels. We are meant to be New Covenant vessels moving in a *New Way* which can take the hard blows from any storm or seas of circumstances. Why is this? Because we have "His Integrity" as the strength in our rigging lines which keep it stable.

Some years ago I entered a sailboat race on Tampa Bay in Florida. This bay was notorious for sudden squalls and gusty winds in summer storms. This was one of those afternoons and I was caught in a summer squall with winds gusting to some 40-50 knots. There was a lot of scrambling on deck to reef down sails, struggling to stay on course. We couldn't even see the bow of my boat for the blowing rain.

When the storm ceased, the results were amazing. Boats had veered way off course, some had dragged their anchors, and others had run aground. But one boat in particular had been "dismasted." His rigging lines had broken and the mast collapsed to the deck. There are a number of problems that you can recover from rather quickly during a sailboat race, but being dismasted is *not* one of them. The owner of this "self-built" vessel was known for cutting corners in the construction of his boat. He did so with inferior materials in his self-made rigging. Consequently, the integrity of the mast, being compromised, came down. Fortunately, he was not out to sea but close in, where friends could help him.

The point I am making here is that a wise master

builder will use the *finest materials available* for his vessel. His life may depend on it! Could we think it's any different for our spiritual vessel?

> *...a God-fashioned life, a life renewed from the inside and working itself into your conduct as God accurately reproduces his character in you.*
> Eph. 4:24, MSG

Do we really think that by our own efforts we could produce better qualities in our character than those that the Holy Spirit has already placed inside us? When we were *sealed with the Holy Spirit,* we received the "Integrity" of Jesus, the "DNA" of our Heavenly Father.

If our life is held together by self-built characteristics, it may look good on the outside, but it just ends up being surface change or behavior modification. Any change that comes from your will power will only last as long as your power will. Whatever is manifested by your will power, will have to be maintained by your will power. It's really about the inward transformation into the image of Jesus. When we believe right, then we'll live right, without effort. It won't happen by focusing on our outward behavior, but by letting the power of the Holy Spirit change us from within. This inner change is what produces the outward manifestation. Being strengthened

Integrity

by anything other than Jesus' strength and His integrity is compromised integrity."

Unimpaired Integrity

Webster defines integrity as "wholeness, entireness, **unbroken** state. The entire **unimpaired** state of anything."

God wants us to be in a "whole and unbroken state." He wants us free from a life *impaired* by self-imposed rules of performance that can hinder our relationship with Him. True integrity is a fruit of who we are in Christ as a *new creation.*

Isn't it much simpler to trust God's integrity than try to produce our own integrity? Jesus is the author and finisher of our faith and all the gifts that He placed in us. With His lines of integrity supporting our tall and sturdy mast, we can fly "full sails," across any ocean and through any storm of life. Any changes needed in us will take place *during* our *journey*, not by our power or might, but through the "New and Living Way" relationship with our Father.

If a living relationship with God could come by rule-keeping, then Christ died unnecessarily.
Gal. 2:24, MSG

Jesus opened the way for this new relationship with our Father that law and religion could never have provided. It's through the cross that we have been made acceptable and pleasing to God. Knowing Jesus and our Father intimately will persuade our hearts that He delights in us, even though we did nothing to deserve it. That is humbling.

> *Everything that goes into a life of pleasing God has been miraculously given to us by getting to know, personally and intimately, the One [Jesus] who invited us to God. The best invitation we ever received!*
>
> 2 Pet 1:3, MSG

Why not come out into "Blue Water" thinking, where we have the deep intimacy of trusting in Jesus? It's there, on the waters of His unconditional love, that we find the *unimpaired* life of joy, freedom, excitement and where a life of real fun can flow. As God's vessels we're not driven by laws or rules, even our own rules (that's the propulsion of *impaired* human effort). No, we are "wind propelled vessels," by the Spirit of Grace, navigating across a fluid realm. Thankfully, we are no longer under a *religious system* or the *world's system*, which can so easily entwine and ensnare. We are being challenged to come into the deep, to a wonderfully *New Way of Living*.

Integrity

Qualified, Righteous and Free

On the ocean there are no yellow or white lines to designate lanes of traffic. There are no speed signs or stop signs. When we leave the "shallow inland waters" to head out into the "deep blue waters" there is a transition in our thinking and believing that takes place. We will need to overcome the fear of leaving the shallows of an old familiar life of *self-dependency* in order to make our way out into the deep where we'll find a new life of *Jesus dependency*, a place where His unconditional love sets us free.

You see, performance-based relationships do not make for an enjoyable journey. A journey like this will be full of doubt and fear leaving us to wonder, "Have we done everything right, or have we done enough *to be pleasing*?" If we think we have that kind of relationship with God then it will put a burden on our thinking. We'll end up *disqualifying* ourselves from the blessings of God, thinking it's our "do" that actually qualifies us.

What qualifies us is what's been "done" by Jesus. The Father qualified us to become "Sons of God," and be *led* by the power of the Kingdom of Light, not *driven* by the domain of darkness.

...giving thanks to the Father, who has qualified us to share in the inheritance of the saints in Light.
Col. 1:12, NAS

We're no longer under the darkness of condemnation and guilt from self-reliance failures. We're in the Light of the saints, through the obedience of Christ at the Cross, not by our obedience or our *earned* self-righteousness (like that of the Pharisees). We've been given the *unearned gift* of righteousness through the Cross and His unmerited favor, providing protection and blessings wherever we sail.

For it is You who blesses the righteous man, O Lord, You surround him with favor as with a shield.
Ps. 5:12, NAS

We are complete in Him. We are righteous, blessed, favored and protected in Him. We already have His integrity. So, let's not get entangled again in a world's system of performance, trying to produce a counterfeit fruit of integrity. That brings us back into dangerous "shallow water thinking." Why would we ever want to go back to the bondage of the law to be a slave again to our "old self?"

Integrity

Entangled

The world's system of "performance mentality" has crept into the Church under the guise of "religion" and seeks to interweave itself into the lives of believers to ensnare them. I am not saying that we separate ourselves from the world. We have to live in the world's system, but the world's system doesn't have to live in us. Jesus said that we are *in* this world but not *of* the world. Haven't we seen ministries fail because they were founded on their own self-effort or "works integrity." Our character is a fruit of our relationship with our Abba Father, not with self.

> *Stand fast therefore in the liberty by which Christ has made us free, and do not be **entangled** again with a yoke of **bondage**.*
>
>   Gal. 5:1, NKJ [emphasis mine]

Paul warns us in Romans 7 to remain divorced from the Law and it's way of thinking. We have been set free from a rule-dominated way of life to be married to another, that is to Jesus and His resurrection life, so that we might bear fruit to God. Coming back into relationship with the Law is really spiritual adultery and the enemy will use it to entangle us again into a yoke of bondage. Entangle means to "entwine, ensnare, or interweave in a manner not easily separated from."

I remember sailing through the Florida Keys about sunset. I decided to take a shorter course through the backwater shallows of the intracoastal waterway. That was a mistake! Suddenly, my vessel came to about half speed and I was having difficulty steering! I couldn't figure out the problem and I was heading towards dangerously shallow waters. I quickly dropped all my sails and looked back off the stern of my vessel. My rudder had *snagged* the buoy line of a lobster trap and I was drifting into the shallows. I frantically worked at getting untangled, managing to do so just in time to head back out into deeper waters.

Being ensnared in anything that pulls your vessel off course, heading you towards the shallows, is not a fun experience. This is why we guard our hearts, because out of our hearts flow the issues of our life. What we focus on becomes what we believe, which will, in turn, set our course heading. Jesus warned us about the "leaven of the Pharisees," meaning their religious, legalistic thinking. Leaven, when it's put into a lump of dough, will work its way through the whole loaf of bread. In other words, if we let legalism, religiosity, or self effort become a part of our belief system, then everything we believe will be affected by that leaven. We've fallen from the Grace Gospel into law mentality. To remain in His peace, we

Integrity

need to understand that "we are *justified* by *faith*, not by *works*."

Therefore, having been justified by faith, we have peace with God through our Lord Jesus Christ, through whom also we have access by faith into this grace in which we stand, and rejoice in hope of the glory of God.

Rom. 5:1, NKJ

The Anchor of Hope

Peace follows us as we focus on Jesus and what He has done. However, *condemnation* follows us if we focus on our "to do list," resulting in *self-righteousness*. This world's system of thinking produces condemnation.

In the Hebrews 4:11 we are instructed to "labor" to enter the "rest" of God lest any man should fall into unbelief. What unbelief? Unbelief in the *finished work of Christ*, in what He provided for us through the "Cross and His Resurrection." This is how we've received every spiritual blessing [Eph. 1:3]. So let's relax and *rest* in God's integrity. Then we can have that assurance and confidence that He has "*garrisoned*" His protection around our life and our character. And that, mate, brings hope and peace. Hope is the anchor for our soul, anchored directly to Jesus.

Jesus at the Helm

*[Now] we have this [**hope**] as a sure and steadfast **anchor** of the soul [it cannot slip and it cannot break down under whoever steps out upon it-] ...that reaches...within the veil.*

Heb. 6:19, AMP

Let me quickly talk about an "anchor." On one occasion I had anchored in the leeward of a Caribbean island just a short distance off a rocky shore, to find shelter from a hard blowing wind. I woke up to the frantic voice of a friend on a nearby sailboat, yelling to me, "You're dragging anchor!" I jumped up and saw that my boat was almost on the rocks. It was obvious that my anchor had broken loose from the bottom. What a panicky feeling! I was scrambling to move my boat away from the rocks. You see, I had failed to pay attention to where I set my anchor. I had set it in a loose, sandy bottom. When the winds picked up, the anchor broke loose and put my boat and crew in danger. This time I reset my anchor in grassy, solid ground where my *anchor could hold* and I could regain my *peace*.

The bible says we're anchored into Jesus. He is steadfast, unshakeable and cannot slip or break down. It's our anchor of hope in Jesus, the confident expectation of good, that brings peace. We are no longer anchored into the sandy, loose ground of self-reliance.

We have a new hope and it keeps our lines of integrity

taut, as well. It works much like a "turnbuckle" on a rigging line that keeps it tight.

*The lines of purpose in your lives never grow slack, tightly tied as they are to your future in heaven, kept taut by **hope**.*
Col.1:5, MSG [emphasis mine]

There's no slack and no compromise in trusting in His divine integrity. It's so simple a child gets it. It takes an adult to make it difficult. Maybe you've been wondering about this integrity business and how it manifests in your life. Let's look and Noah Webster's definition of trust:

Confidence; a reliance or *resting of the mind* on the **integrity**, **veracity**, justice, **friendship** or other sound principle of *another person.*

When our minds rest in the integrity and character of Jesus, the result of trusting in Him is that our confidence and faith *soars*. We have peace of mind that just happens effortlessly. Everything He is, we are [1 John 4:17]. When we focus on His integrity, on His "veracity" [truthfulness], it manifests in us. God built us to *become like what we focus on* with our hearts. So, we can rest our minds in the intimate, trustworthy, friendship of Jesus. And as a fruit of trusting in Him, His character begins to manifest in us.

Lets ask the Holy Spirit to show us which lines of integrity we're depending on. Are they the New Covenant lines of integrity in Jesus, which are living, pliable, tight and unbreakably strong rigging? Or are they Old Covenant integrity that is hard, brittle, loose fitting, legalistic, self-reliant, compromised, breakable, rigging? Which rigging do you want holding your mast through the storms of life?

The Great Exchange

Jesus paid a high price to purchase the gifts we've been given and the freedom to use them. He "spoiled" the enemy and gave us the same power to spoil the enemy!

*And having **spoiled** principalities and powers, he made a show of them openly, triumphing over them in it.*

Col. 2:15, KJV [emphasis mine]

The Strong's Concordance defines spoil as "to pillage" or "to sink." This is a great picture of how Jesus triumphed over the enemy, pillaging and sinking the devil's boat. He did it openly when he rose from the grave and appeared to many, proving He had conquered

Integrity

the last enemy, death. So often we've read verse 15 above, and shouted, "Yea! Jesus spoiled principalities and powers!" But, we miss verse 14, telling us *how* Jesus spoiled principalities and powers.

> *Blotting out the handwriting of **ordinances** that was against us, which was contrary to us, and took it out of the way, **nailing** it to the **cross**;*
> Col. 2:14, KJV [emphasis mine]

These were legal rights of the Law and Commandments to hold sins and transgressions against us, used by the enemy to keep us in bondage. Jesus took the enemy's number one weapon that kept us in bondage under condemnation, guilt, shame, feeling unworthy, and nailed it to the cross forever. That's how Jesus pillaged and sank the devil's boat. The strong man is bound. His house has been plundered. Hallelujah!

Interestingly enough, one of the root words of "spoiled," in Col. 2:15, is the word "reversal." Through the Cross of Christ we see that when Jesus spoiled the enemy, He reversed the position for all those who would believe. By His Grace we've received the "Great Exchange," that is, He took our sin and shame, we got His righteousness and no condemnation. He took our disease, pain and sorrow; we got His health, joy and happiness. He took our chastisement and we got His peace. He became poor and, through Him, we became rich. He took our lack and poverty; in exchange, He gave us provision and riches from His glory.

Old Covenant religion and performance thinking of what we "must do" was exchanged at the Cross for the New Covenant Grace Gospel of what Jesus "has done." It's all been done for us. It's such good news that we have a hard time wrapping our minds around it. It's the New Way of seeing ourself operating in His extravagant Grace.

Mostly what God does is love you. Keep company with him and learn a life of love. Observe how Christ loved us. His love was not cautious but extravagant.
Eph. 5:1, MSG

Focus on Jesus and let His Integrity manifest from within. It will seem almost effortless because we become like what we focus on. It's part of our DNA from the Father. As I've already said earlier, the first words I heard from the Father were, "God is fun!" I have fed on those three words for years and still haven't sailed to the end of them yet. Hey mate, I haven't arrived, but I've hoisted my sails, set His course, and I'm underway on an appointed journey. Our God is a radically adventurous, exciting, and fun God!

Let's set sail with Jesus and go for it!

Integrity

Chapter 7

Your Barometer

*I am training you son to listen and listen **carefully**. If you're having difficulty hearing your mate, you will be having difficulty hearing the voice of the Holy Spirit. So listen with understanding to what she says and what she feels. I've made her as a "barometer" on board My Vessel. She may at times feel a "storm" ahead in the spiritual, the same as a barometer reads "air pressure" to tell you if good or bad weather is ahead in the natural. I've given her a sensitivity to My Spirit to be able to sense good or bad weather ahead. When she describes something she is feeling, don't ask her for an explanation to satisfy your reasoning mind. I speak to hearts, not to reasoning minds.*

*It is My desire that you work together as a team, a crew finely fit together, taking your positions on board. So listen and move in **faith** not in **reasoning**.*

I will put in her a sense of when I'm stirring the waters, to get ready for a move. Even though you've

Your Barometer

found a good anchorage, it doesn't mean that my plan for you is to stay in that anchorage or that "safe harbor" indefinitely. I may be calling you to pull up anchor and come out into the "deep." I will put a stirring in her, my son, to know a time is at hand to move out of that anchorage. Be ready, instant in season and out of season. Be ready to "set sail," to move where My Spirit will lead you both.

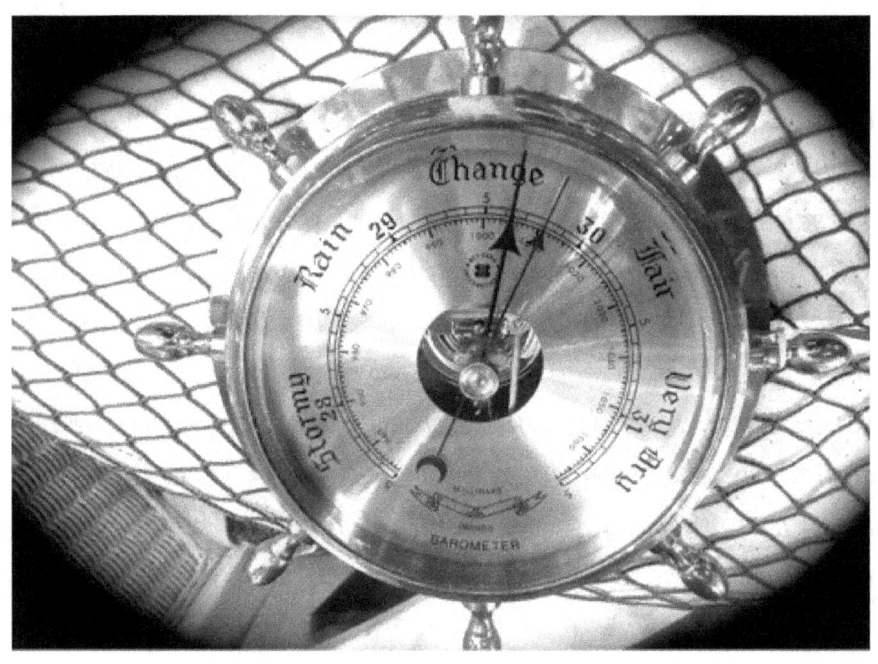

Jesus at the Helm

A Rib for a Bride

I need to begin this chapter with a bit of a notation. Every person has their own personal voyage that they are on, as the chapters in this book make evident. However, in this particular chapter we'll be speaking about the vessel where both husband and wife are a team, learning to operate in their callings. Having said that, let me begin.

This is one of the more difficult chapters for me to write or I should say to understand, probably because I am still so much in the learning stage of this message. In any case, I know it's true from experience and from the Word. I know I am probably taking a fat chance writing this chapter and may get some comments in response, but I do believe it needs to be said. So lets look at the Word:

And the rib, which the Lord God had taken from man, made he a woman, and brought her unto the man... Therefore shall a man leave his father and his mother, and shall cleave unto his wife; and they shall be one flesh.

Gen. 2:22, 24; KJV

Here we see a couple of important events. It was not just the rib that man was missing from that point forward, but much of what went into the creation of the woman –

motherly love, care, certain emotions and supernatural sensitivity, etc. And there are certain things the man was created with that are not in the woman. Where one is weak, the other can be strong and together they can operate as one unit in a sense of rhythm as joint heirs. I believe this is why the Holy Spirit makes it clear that when He brings the two into one whole unit, the man *leaves* and *cleaves*. Paul quotes the scripture above and goes on to say in Eph. 5:32 that this is a great mystery concerning Christ and the Church. This is the only other relationship that parallels our relationship with Jesus Christ, the Groom and His love for each one of us, His bride, the Church.

Now, here I have to "heave to" and make a few needed comments. First, we are talking about the godly union of a man and a woman. No man or woman can fulfill the vacuum in a person that only God can fulfill. If you expect a spouse or mate to fulfill only what God can, you are already headed for problems.

In the case of a marriage where only one spouse is a believer, God still operates in that home supernaturally through the life of the believer on behalf of the spouse and the lives of the children to set them apart.

For the unbelieving husband is sanctified by the wife, and the unbelieving wife is sanctified by the husband; else were your children unclean; but now are they holy.

1 Cor. 7:14, NKJ

If you are a believer, headed towards a marital relationship with an unbeliever, that could be a mistake. The bible warns about being unequally yoked together with unbelievers. I've prayed with many a spouse that went ahead in a marriage to an unbeliever, thinking they could change the person or the situation. Not good thinking. If you're one who is already in that relationship, then trust God. Jesus can breathe life into any situation that seems impossible and turn it around for the good by His Grace.

Second, you can read what Paul says concerning those called to celibacy in 1 Cor. 7, either man or woman. In that case, it is God who will complete that person for we are complete in Christ. There is therefore no stigma for those who feel God has called them to be celibate.

Sensitivity or Crazy

Let's return now to barometers. Barometers differ in looks, sizes and shapes, but the most common you will see is the round gauge with a needle as the indicator. In

Your Barometer

this chapter I am talking about how a wife has a "sensitivity" much like a barometer. The barometer basically measures the weight of air mass at its location. For a sailor, it would be at sea level which is the standard pressure. It's purpose is to measure barometric pressure and tell you when the air pressure is rising or falling. That information, in turn, tells us if cloudy, rainy weather is forming and possibly a storm, or if sunny, good weather is on the horizon.

I said all that to say this. The barometer reads and measures forces that cannot be felt or seen. How does this pertain to women? I believe God has placed in women a certain instinct or sensitivity that often cannot be felt or seen by men. Often wives may feel things, such as a sort of nesting instinct that tells them it may be time to drop anchor and set up a home or pull up anchor and relocate. In other words, she often has a sensitivity to when it's time to set up and when it's time to take down. I believe this is a godly instinct working inside her. Sometimes she may feel uneasy or threatened, possibly by something on the horizon that could be threatening to the home both in the spiritual and in the natural. That, my friend, would be "bad weather or a storm." It could be anything from a financial situation to a family problem concerning the children. Maybe she feels the presence of an intruder on the horizon. Perhaps another woman may have an eye on her husband. Hmm!

Maybe it's time to "tack" and change course.

In any case, she is very much like a barometer. She may feel Son-shine ahead, an encouragement to stay on course, even though it may currently be gloomy and overcast. On the other hand, your barometer may be saying that it's time to come into port to set the anchor. She may be feeling bad weather ahead, over the horizon, even when it looks sunny and clear. If it was me, I believe I would start praying and checking the charts for a "Port of Rest."

Now, please don't take this to the extreme and think I'm saying the wife replaces the Holy Spirit. I'm just saying we help and encourage one another as a gift from God, and a barometer is a GOOD gift that brings favor.

*He who finds a wife finds a **good** thing, And obtains **favor** from the Lord.*
Prov. 18:22, NKJ [emphasis mine]

God has put this "barometric sense" in a woman and she may not even understand it herself. So, when she expresses something she feels, don't take it lightly, but take it to the Lord. All I am saying is that if she feels a storm on the horizon and you don't pay attention to that warning, then you won't be prepared when a storm suddenly hits your vessel. Well, my friend, your bacon is gonna be burnt and her barometric pressure readings may reach a new high.

In those times, when a woman is not able to express what she is feeling, it could be that the husband is not the least bit aware that something is on the horizon. Maybe he's just not focused and been missing it while the Holy Spirit has been trying to get his attention for a course change. Being men, however, we like to hear logical explanations of what our spouse is feeling and why she feels that way. She may not have a logical explanation or her reasoning is totally out of the realm of understanding for a man. Either way, when it is not logical it just kind of short circuits a man's brain. As men we need to hear more from our heart than from logical thinking.

Often, Old Testament scriptures have been wrongly used by ministers to discourage New Covenant believers from listening to their hearts. Today, through the new birth under the new covenant of Grace, we have received a new SPIRIT and a new HEART.

I'll give you a new heart, put a new spirit in you. I'll remove the stone heart from your body and replace it with a heart that's God-willed, not self-willed. I'll put my Spirit in you...

Ez. 36:26, MSG

Jesus at the Helm

On Hearts Not Tablets

As sons of God, we are totally a new creation. God has come to indwell the New Covenant believer and put His desires and promptings in their hearts.

> *For it is God which worketh in you both to will and to do of his good pleasure.*
>
> Phil. 2:13, KJV

In our New Covenant Grace Gospel, God writes His plan on our hearts. So now it's with our hearts that we are learning to hear from God.

> *...This time "I'm writing out the plan in them, carving it on the lining of their hearts."*
>
> Heb. 10:16, MSG

Jesus said His sheep hear His voice and a stranger's voice they will not follow. In our hearts we will hear His voice but we have to learn to recognize it. I believe that as we learn to hear from our mate at the heart level, we also learn to hear more easily from God at the heart level.

Jesus so often said, "Let him who has ears to hear, let him hear." I believe He is talking about hearing at the heart level. Salvation is hearing at the heart level. In Romans 10 it says that if you confess with your mouth and believe in your *heart* that God raised Jesus from the dead, you shall be saved. I do believe Jesus has us in training, learning to listen with our hearts as we spend time with Him.

There is more to becoming *one flesh* than just flesh. Heart level communication is how we learn to work in harmony with our mate as a single unit. Speaking from the heart is being transparent with no obstacles in the way.

To be in unity with our spouse we need to be flowing together in a rhythm of peace and rest. That's how we learn to take our right positions on board. The two have become one on board, flowing together as a crew and as mates. We will go through some rough waters learning to operate in unity. We will have disagreements, but learning not to let ourselves come under condemnation is extremely important.

The Lord spoke to me once and said, "Son, it doesn't matter to Me so much who is right or who is wrong when you both have a fuss. Just keep peace on board and I will bring things around to work out for the good." I say this with a slight lump in my throat. He also said to me, "Be the first to apologize."

Jesus at the Helm

*Be eager and strive earnestly to guard and keep the **harmony** and oneness of [and produced by] the Spirit in the **binding** power of **peace**.*

Eph. 4:3, AMP [emphasis mine]

God understands that we have disagreements on board and that's okay, but He doesn't want us to come under condemnation about it. We have to understand that we are still "right" with God. Just make up and let Him sort out the differences. This is how to avoid "mutiny" on board and make sure no one ends up "walking the gang plank."

So, if you and your spouse have an argument, get rid of strife as quick as possible, just repent, that is change your mind. That means, my brother, you'll probably have to apologize. Don't try to work this out in your own strength as that will put you under the law and produce *death* that could run you aground. Bring the relationship back to the Spirit of Grace and let His power work it out.

Reading Your Barometer

Let's talk about some characteristics of the barometer. At the beginning of this chapter, you may have noticed a picture of a barometer with words and numbers on the face. Notice the three words, "Rain, Change, and Fair," that are peculiar to the barometer, with a needle to

Your Barometer

indicate the reading. The barometer [wife] that God gave to us men, may not be quite that easy to read. It would be nice if we could look at our wife's face and see something that would indicate, "Aha, fair skies ahead." Or maybe, "Uh oh, there's rain in the forecast, but is it a light pitter patter rain or "It's a thunderstorm with high winds!" The good news is that the word "change" appears on the barometer. Whatever the present circumstances are, just know it will change.

Understanding comes with time as we pursue our relationship. Since each barometer [wife] has her own peculiar heart voice, husbands need to better learn how to listen to that heart voice. In turn, we'll be better equipped to hear and understand the voice of the Holy Spirit.

Husbands, likewise, dwell with them with understanding,

1 Peter 3:7, NKJ

This learning how to read and understand our barometer is the key to spending more time in "fair weather sailing."

A barometer is a delicate instrument and, in the natural, needs to be in a *protected* area on any boat. When out to sea, there is salt spray flying from waves and hitting the hull of the boat, resulting in sea salt covering everything. After a short time you kind of feel like a "salt lick." This is why the barometer needs to be in a clean, sheltered place on a voyage.

In the spiritual realm, it is the same. Husbands have been instructed to love their wives as Christ did the Church, to protect them from harmful elements, and to wash her with the water of the Word. That is the Good News Gospel.

> *Husbands, love your wives, just as Christ also loved the church and gave Himself for her, that He might sanctify and cleanse her with the **washing** of **water** by the word.*
>
> Eph. 5:25-26, NKJ [emphasis mine]

The "washing" is not only speaking the Word over our wives, but *living it out in Love.*

> *...Be good husbands to your wives. Honor them, delight in them. As women they lack some of your advantages. But in the new life of God's grace, you're **equals**. Treat your wives, then, as equals so your prayers don't **run aground**.*
>
> 1 Pet. 3:7, MSG [emphasis mine]

Wives are relational and want to know they are joint heirs and equals with their mates on this Grace journey.

Your Barometer

Let's "heave to" momentarily and dispel some wrong doctrine about prayers "running aground." When we have disagreements or problems between us and our spouse, *our prayers can run aground* if we let ourselves come under condemnation and guilt. God does not refuse to hear our prayers or cause the "heavens to become brass." Because of the finished work of Jesus at the Cross, He opened the heavens forever, for all believers. When we're having problems, that's the exact time our Abba Father wants us to come to Him in prayer. The enemy uses strife and division to make both the husband and wife feel unworthy or disqualified to come to Him in prayer. He tries to make us feel alienated from God. That's how prayers run aground. We fail to come to God because of those unworthy feelings of condemnation. We get stuck in shallow waters and begin to live a life of defeat. God doesn't want us to live a "sin conscious" life but rather a "Son conscious" life. The way out of those waters is to turn your focus back onto Jesus and your right standing with Him. The Holy Spirit will get your vessel off that sand bar and back into the blue waters.

Wives are also natural "responders." They reciprocate when they're receiving love and honor.

Jesus at the Helm

...this provides a good picture of how each husband is to treat his wife, loving himself in loving her, and how each wife is to honor her husband.

Eph. 5:33, MSG

Just as a barometer responds to air pressure, wives respond to husbands loving and honoring them. Knowing that our barometer [wife] responds to pressure, then it would be in our best interest to keep the pressure *light* by loving our wives and treating them with respect. That could produce a smiley face on the barometer and make for fair weather sailing ahead. Conversely, heavy, burdensome pressure could mean a rainy or stormy day ahead.

When both husband and wife are in harmony flowing together, I believe there will be a change in relationships and in "barometric pressure." Change only comes as we focus on the ship's Captain [Jesus]. I'd much rather deal with a *storm outside* the vessel than deal with a *storm on board* the vessel which may lead to a possible mutiny. Let's keep our barometers in good working order.

Through the Cross, Jesus made one nation in a day. Jews and Gentiles became *one new man* in Christ. Through the Cross, husband and wife are "one flesh," or "one new crew" through the Spirit. Working together, they are a powerful vessel in the Lord's Fleet, a crew finely fit together in harmony, sailing a journey never thought possible. God has placed many good gifts in all our lives, but as men we are to remember that our barometer is the good gift. We need to lift our wives up and encourage them in their gifting and who they are in Christ. We have been *blessed* with a wife that has special gifts and talents.

> *House and riches are the inheritance from fathers, but a wise, understanding, and prudent wife is from the Lord.*
> Prov. 19:14, AMP

Jesus has given us as *gifts to each other*, to be His arms of Love, to bring healing, hope and freedom to one another. He wants us to be whole and free, even more than we want to be. Free to be ourselves. Free from condemnation and guilt. Free from self accusing thoughts that kill our relationship with God and our spouse. We cannot have the freedom of a good relationship if we think the person is angry with us. It will actually stop the "wind of your destiny."

> *...as I swore that the waters of Noah should no more go over the earth, so I have sworn that I will not be angry with you, and will not rebuke you.*
> Is. 54:9, ESV

Jesus at the Helm

God put His rainbow in the sky as His signature to declare to His vessels that He will never rebuke or be angry with us. We are always under His sky of Peace. Our Abba Father is always GOOD and does only good to us. If it's bad, it's not God. We are His new and living way crew, born anew to be conscious of His Love written on our hearts.

We love because he first loved us.
                              John 4:19, ESV

For us to find intimacy with Jesus and our Abba Father, God first had to shed His Love abroad in our hearts by the Holy Spirit. He wants to bring an experiential manifestation to our hearts, so real that we cannot deny the presence of His Love in us. He wants us to know His Love for us as part of the family in the Kingdom of God. As we become more conscious of His Love, our faith is activated to *respond* by the *resting of our minds* in His integrity, veracity and friendship.

As I've said many times now, we are on a journey of discovery, learning to trust in Him so we become trustworthy with our spouse and others. Letting His Love, goodness, integrity and friendship flow out of us, we can share intimately with our spouse as best friends and best lovers on this Grace Journey.

Your Barometer

Let the peace of Christ keep you in tune with each other, in step with each other. None of this going off and doing your own thing. And cultivate thankfulness.
Col. 3:15, MSG

We are on this journey, learning to work together in peace and harmony, becoming one on a voyage of great mystery. He wants us to relax and enjoy His presence, His friendship and His fellowship as our trusted Captain.

Now that we are sailing these New Covenant Waters, we feel a fresh new wind. This wind of the Holy Spirit is revealing to us who we are in Christ as *joint heirs* and that we are *partners* on our journey together. Let's learn to rest and enjoy the scenery as we sail through these fluid blue waters in the rhythm of His Grace.

He is making us "two as one." This is His real freedom!

Chapter 8

Spiritual Doldrums

There will be times when you will sail into Spiritual Doldrums. This is a very important time, so be patient and remain in the confident expectation of good that I will bring to you. Let not your heart be troubled. Yes, it's not comfortable as seas continue rolling in to rock your vessel from "port to starboard" [side to side] with no wind in the sails to steady her. You've arrived at a place where the wind has laid down, ceased, and it may seem almost frightening.

*This is the time, however, when My vessels should be learning to wait upon Me, and I say it again, "Wait upon Me." It's here that many can make the mistake of relying on their reasoning mind, their flesh. They say, "I know the course heading our God wants us on. Let's turn on our auxiliary engine [the flesh] and follow **our** plan. Let's take up **our** course, **we** will **find** the wind." So, they begin to motor through seas under their own strength, using up the fuel of their own energy, with no wind in the* sails to steady their vessel. They say, "See, we are making headway," but without wind to steady their vessel, they plunge their bows into the seas ahead. They take on "waves of discouragement," in their own strength. Those on board begin to feel ill, and those that continue on, insisting that they are making headway and are "on course," find out later that they've missed My Wind. They've veered off course and the crew is sick, tired, discouraged and worn out. Not learning from this, so often they begin looking for a "port of call" where they can go in for an "upgrade." They say, "We just need a bigger engine [more flesh], so we can move faster and make better headway." It's during these times that the enemy arrives to cause derision and division, introducing course changes of deception.

Others however, will come to the end of themselves and give up their own ways to turn to Me for help. This will be a time of revelation and blessing for them. I will work things together for their good to get them back on My course and moving by the Wind of My Spirit.

But you are **My Vessel** created to move by the power of **My Wind**, not by the power of the **flesh**. I say, be patient and listen for My Wind. Focus on Me and know this is only **temporary**. Check with the mate I have given you and discern the weather together. Use this time to receive My Word and let it go down deep into your vessel with the rest of the "heavenly ballast" I've placed in you.

Jesus at the Helm

This is a time for praise and joy. The winds will surely come again and you will be better prepared as a vessel ready to move out on the winds from heaven.

*Your vessel will stay on "her foot" [upright], moving out swiftly under sail with a cool breeze blowing across her deck on a steady, comfortable ride. Then you will see that the winds have changed and are now coming from a **different** direction. It's time now to set your sails accordingly and to make a course change. It will be a change in course from that of **old traditions** to **A New Covenant** course heading. Don't worry, I know the best course heading and destination for your vessel. I have undiscovered secrets and treasures ahead for you. Pay no attention to those vessels that move out under their own power. Rather, pay attention to the course I have laid before you, and the direction of the winds I have given you. You have not lost time, for I redeem the time! Oh! Listen for My Wind! Put your face into this Wind. Feel it, smell it. This wind carries a new fragrance. It's the sweet aroma of your trust in Me. Now, set your sails, and steady as you go!*

Spiritual Doldrums

Oh No! Doldrums

Doldrums are defined as "belts of very still air" and are a natural consequence of wind currents, high and low pressures, with little to no wind. They commonly occur near the equator but can also occur anywhere between the Tropics in the Atlantic, Pacific, and Indian Oceans. They were noted for stalling out sailing ships of old, for days and sometimes even weeks.

In the natural, sailing into doldrums can be uncanny and unsettling, seeming almost like a supernatural event. It's not uncommon to see winds going flat for short periods of time between rain cells or wind shifts, but when the breeze goes away for a day or longer, I call that a "doldrum."

Jesus at the Helm

On one trip I was sailing east to Jamaica from Mexico and little did I know I was headed directly into some huge seas that were rolling down from a hurricane spawned off the coast of Trinidad. It was a good distance away but with no land between, I found myself punching into 25 foot seas with such hard breakers at the top that it caused my vessel to "judder" under the force of the impact. The next moment I would be white knuckled at the helm, surfing down the back side of those waves which were throwing a sheet of salt spray over me and the boat. Finally, after long hours of tense sailing, I made landfall. I spent several days there, still rocking on my "sea legs" while trying to recover from fatigue. By that time, the seas had returned to normal. I restocked my boat for a hopefully easy return trip to Mexico. I set sail with the prevailing winds on my stern. To my amazement, there was a drastic change in the winds on this leg of the journey. The breeze went from slack, to suddenly no breeze at all.

The waves kept rolling in for awhile and it was one ugly ride with no wind in the sails to steady my boat. She would roll port to starboard and rock bow to stern like a hobby horse. It was uncomfortable to say the least. Sailboats today are equipped with auxiliary engines, quite different from the old square riggers equipped only with oars. Still, sailboats do not ride well motoring through swells and no wind in the sails to steady her.

Spiritual Doldrums

That's a ride that can cause anyone on board, with a tendency toward sea sickness, to end up hanging over the side of the vessel releasing their last meal.

To my amazement, the seas went flat as mirrored glass. As far as I could see, there was not a cloud in the sky, and not a ripple on the sea. I had never in my life seen the oceans this smooth. To my dismay, I had sailed into a doldrum. Wow! The silence was deafening. Conditions on the sea can change quickly and unexpectedly. One of those conditions is a doldrum.

We can pass through a doldrum in the spiritual realm as well. Everything seems to come to a halt, but God has not left us there alone. Our answer is still the same – keep your focus on Jesus and do not get into fret or worry. Instead, let God have all your anxious thoughts and feelings. Let not your heart be troubled!

Give all your worries and cares to God, for he cares about you.
                                    1 Peter 5:7, NLT

Flesh or Spirit

Let's look at a comparison between spiritual sailing vessels moved by the power of the *wind* and those moved by the power of the *flesh*. As vessels in the Kingdom of God, we are created to be moved by the Wind of the Holy

Spirit. But some sailing vessels use their auxiliary engines of "flesh power" to push their vessel through the seas of life, *reasoning* that they know the course God wants.

However, making headway to any destination by our "flesh power" rather than "Holy Spirit power" is a hard, uncomfortable ride for any crew or mate.

In the natural, if I sailed into a doldrum, one of the first things I would want is to find a place of shade on board. I'd stretch out a canvas awning over the cockpit to escape the Caribbean sun, kind of like Jonah sitting under a leafy plant for shade, waiting for something to happen.

In our spiritual life, sailing into a doldrum can feel a bit uncanny, like we're stuck and unable to make any headway. We begin to look for shade from the heat and stagnancy of the circumstances. It's not a time to fall into inactivity, but rather Spirit-led activity. Just know you are not stagnant and you will pass through. This is the time to keep focused on Jesus and praise Him.

Because you have been my help, therefore in the shadow of Your wings I will rejoice.
Ps. 63:7, NKJ

In Jesus we find a place of shade, protection, and favor while rejoicing under the shadow of His Wings. At times it may seem formidable, even unbearable, surrounded by the thunder of silence and the stillness of circumstances. It's not unusual to wonder if God is even around when going through a spiritual doldrum, or to wonder if the enemy has tricked us into this place of silence. Know that Jesus has not left us, nor has He put us on a shelf.

This is an important time and place in our spiritual life where we are learning to *wait upon the Lord*. One of our most challenging efforts is to *cease* from our own efforts and *rest* totally in Jesus! If we focus on Jesus, it will free us from being anxious or despondent and lead us into rejoicing and thanksgiving. We may feel like a "bobber" on the ocean, but God is there with us. Seen from God's point of view, this is not a problem, but a time of celebration and an opportunity to worship Him.

Let Go and Rest!

*There remaineth therefore a **rest** to the people of God. For he that is entered into **his** rest, he also hath ceased from his **own works**...*
Heb. 4:9-10, KJV [emphasis mine]

A doldrum, seen in a positive way, could be the place to get us back into the flow of Grace. It may be a place where we've come to the *end of ourselves.* Sometimes it's the only way we will let go of our self-effort course so the Holy Spirit can put us on His Grace course. It can be a place to lose our old identity. Pull down the banner of "Self-Effort" to hoist the new banner, "At Rest While God Works."

This is often a place where we "let go and let God," so we can fully enjoy this sailing adventure. Let's make use of the doldrum to learn how to rest in God, to communicate with our mate, and to enjoy the trip. It can also be a time to get into the flow of the Spirit, a time of drawing together, not apart, a time to *sit at the feet* of Jesus and let His Word go deep into our "keel" [heart]. One of the hardest things for us to do, is to *sit down*. Let's take time to let the Holy Spirit renew our dreams and visions. As we do, our life will prosper.

In a doldrum, it may seem like we've arrived at the edge of the world, a place where we either fall off or turn around and go back. But this could be the place where we are humbled by the realization that *we need help*. Either Jesus does it or we're not gonna make it.

I've tried everything and nothing helps. I'm at the end of my rope. Is there no one who can do anything for Me? Isn't that the real question? The answer, thank God, is that Jesus Christ can and does.
Rom. 7:24-25, MSG

Spiritual Doldrums

Our answer is always Jesus and He has already planned a course to move us out of this doldrum. We don't need to work up a sweat through self-effort to push our vessel out of here by our own energy. God is not the One who led us into these doldrums. I believe it's usually our own self-effort plan that put us off course and into a doldrum.

A man's heart deviseth his way; but the Lord directeth his steps.

Prov. 16:9, KJV

Whatever the reason, our answer is always to trust in Him and He will get us back on course. It's God's delight to work in us and direct our course by His Spirit, as we rest in Him. The Holy Spirit will comfort us and remind us that even in the middle of this doldrum, we are right with God and not to worry, we are unique and have been given gifts that are unique. He will lead us out of worry and fret, regardless of the circumstances. Trusting in Him is a sweet savor unto God.

I believe God uses this time to work something special in us, to separate us from an old life of works, religion, and traditions of men. It may even feel like an umbilical cord is being cut, freeing us from an old belief system. It's like an old "sea anchor" being severed from our vessel that we've unknowingly been dragging around so long that it seemed natural. We are being separated from the dead things that have clung to our vessel. This sailing journey is revealing more of the New Grace Sovereign Realm which brings us a new life of freedom. Our new identity is a Christ-centered, grace rhythmic, refreshed new self. I hope you are catching my point. We are being set free from the bondage of self, which is actually 180 degrees off course.

> *The person who lives in right relationship with God does it by embracing what God arranges for him. Doing things for God is the **opposite** of entering into what God does for you.*
>
> Gal. 3:12, MSG [emphasis mine]

You see, doing things *for* God to be right with Him puts us back under the law. The enemy tries to use a doldrum to get us back under the law and isolate us from God. He wants to get us into self examination, trying to figure out why we are in this doldrum. Becoming introspective by looking to *self* for answers only invites *condemnation*. We'll likely start blaming ourselves and others (like our mate) for the circumstances we find ourselves in. That, my friend, is a course headed for the "Port of Division." Sadly, condemnation will make us run *from* God, not *to* God.

Spiritual Doldrums

Who to Follow

In the spiritual realm, it will be tempting to follow after those other vessels that fire up their auxiliary engines of flesh. We see their vessels moving out and it appears that they are making headway. But if their vessel is not on God's course and His plan, it doesn't matter that they are moving, they are *not* making headway. They'll likely end up powering through seas of life, with no wind in their sails to steady her, and plunging their bows into waves of discouragement. It will end up being a ride fueled by *self strategy*, on a course destined for *burn out*, headed for the "Harbor of Disappointment."

> *There are many out there taking other paths, choosing other goals, and trying to get you to go along with them. ...All they want is easy street. They hate Christ's Cross.*
>
> Phil. 3:18, MSG

It's a mistake to give in to the temptation to follow someone else's course heading just to feel like we are moving. Whatever we initiate by flesh power, we have to maintain by flesh power. However, if those vessels will give it up and let go to let God introduce them to His rest, they'll find a refreshing. He will *save* them from their own hard labors, enabling them to be a *restful*, not a *fearful* vessel. Remember, we're *led* not *driven*.

Sadly, some will not give heed to the cost of the labor and stress of a self-effort course. They continue on, looking for ways to add more flesh power to an already tiresome journey. Often competitive, ambitious, and full of themselves, they reason that success and the blessings of God come by self-effort power. But success is not good success unless it's God's success.

This is when Satan's ship, "Condemnation," shows up on the horizon. He is a nefarious pirate, searching for a vessel to release his law weapons on. Jealousy, ridicule, contempt will bring division and derision on board. He can't take our treasure, so he will try to take us out of commission by driving us off our Grace Course. He uses religious persecution of vessels around us to bring condemnation, confusion and guilt. He ultimately wants to move our focus from our Christ identity to a self identity, and to leave the leading of the Holy Spirit.

And oh, my dear Timothy, guard the treasure you were given! Guard it with your life. Avoid the talk-show religion and the practiced confusion of the so-called experts. People caught up in a lot of talk can miss the whole point of faith. Overwhelming Grace keep you!
    1 Tim. 6:20-22, MSG

Self focus causes derision and will invite division with our mate. Let's be wise to the wiles of the devil and guard our hearts and relationships with all diligence. Focus on Jesus, the treasures He has given us, and what He has accomplished at the Cross. It will bring us back to our "Grace Course" where our faith remains strong.

Fruit Happens

It's not uncommon to think, as we're passing through a doldrum, that nothing is happening and we're just stagnant. But there is something happening of great value. The truth is, if we'll rest in the Spirit, fruit will be produced in our lives. We're just the branches that abide in the vine (Jesus). He is the One responsible to produce fruit as we let His life flow through us. Hey mate, fruit will just happen.

Even in a doldrum, when it seems we're not moving, fruit can still be produced. *Moving* is not the criteria to produce fruit, but *abiding* is. Trying to produce fruit by our own strength is not abiding, but remaining in His love is abiding. Keep believing who we are in Christ and acknowledging all the good things in us.

Jesus at the Helm

*Blessed is the man who trusts in the Lord, And whose **hope** is the Lord. For he shall be like a tree planted by the waters, Which spreads out its roots by the river, And will not fear when **heat** comes; But its leaf will be green, And will not be anxious in the year of drought, Nor will cease from yielding **fruit**.*

Jer. 17:7-8, NKJ [emphasis mine]

It may appear as though other vessels are doing well at bearing fruit, but don't be deceived and don't enter into competition. If they're trusting in their own power, they are actually squeezing off the life juices from flowing through them. Trying to produce fruit by your own power is as unfruitful as trying to move your vessel by blowing on your sails. The only fruit produced through struggling is *plastic* fruit, the fruit of "behavior modification." It looks good on the *outside,* but it's not real on the *inside.* By us simply putting our trust and hope in Him, *fruit happens*.

Working hard in our own strength, without resting and abiding in the vine, is like chasing the wind. We could end up missing His wind. Besides, it will just wear us down and out. Focus on Jesus, this doldrum is only temporary. So get ready! God doesn't want us stagnant, growing those weeds of discontent on the hull of our vessel. Remain in His rest, expecting a new wind to come. He will not disappoint us. Why? Because we have His favor, an unending supply, including a fresh wind of the Spirit. Let's take this opportunity to receive from Him, gleaning words of life. This is a preparation for the next leg of our journey.

Why Doldrums?

Now, I don't believe God leads us into doldrums, and I'm not saying every vessel has to go through the doldrums like I did, but I just haven't met a mate yet who hasn't encountered the doldrums at some point on their journey. Whatever the reason we find ourself passing through a doldrum, God will use it for our good. Don't let it take you from a course of rest to a course of stress. God can use a doldrum to get us back on course.

As I have said earlier, we will experience lonely times on our voyage, but the good news is that as we let the Holy Spirit lead us through times of loneliness, we'll learn to follow Him and not the crowd. Depend on the Holy Spirit to lead you and not on the influence of the crowd mentality. Let's relax and stop trying to figure it all out on our own. Follow the peace in our hearts!

Jesus at the Helm

And let the peace [soul harmony which comes] from Christ rule [act as umpire continually] in your hearts [deciding and settling with finality all questions that arise in your minds...]"

Col. 3:15, AMP

A New Wind

In the natural, I saw the wind manifest in different ways as I was coming out of a doldrum. I would see wind patterns begin to dance across the surface of the water, first in one area and then in another. They would develop into wind ripples, making patterns on the face of the waters, as if a hand was passing over the surface. Invariably, there would be a change in the wind direction. I would put my face into the wind to smell the fresh ocean breeze. Then I would hear the wind start to ruffle the sails as they began to draw tight, tugging on the "sheeting lines." My boat would lunge forward, accelerating through the water, slightly healed but on her foot. I was off and running, making headway, the bow knifing through the calm seas. What an awesome sight!

In the spiritual realm, it's much the same. The power of an *unseen wind* sweeps across and fills our spiritual sails. Praise and worship, the "Spinnaker Sail" of our heart, fills us with the winds from heaven. The feel of a cool breeze of joy, begins blowing across our sails.

Spiritual Doldrums

There is just something about putting your face into the wind, feeling it's power, and getting a whiff of the fresh air from heaven. It's His wind of abundance and favor that's blowing a fresh breeze across our sails, bringing a new excitement to our hearts!

...He bringeth the wind out of His treasuries.
Ps. 135:7, KJV

When we notice this wind has changed directions, we need to set our sails accordingly. We're about to set sail on a new course and there's a new feeling on this course. There's no more pressure to move by *performance*, we're leaving an old course of dead works behind. We're setting the compass course on a "new and living way." Something has happened in the spiritual realm, and there is a sense of new things on the horizon. There is a knowing in us that Jesus has gone ahead to make provision. We are in His plan and on His course, where things can happen effortlessly. We're on a course for undiscovered treasures and surprises of good things, laid out since the foundations of the world.

Our part, well, it's just to trust Him. He'll never let us down. He's the "Lord of Restoration." He will turn things around and restore all that appears to have been lost. He will even redeem the time and renew our dreams. It's never too late!

Jesus at the Helm

Trust God from the bottom of our heart; don't try to figure out everything on your own. Listen for God's voice in everything you do, everywhere you go; He's the one who will keep you on track.
Prov. 3:5-6, MSG

We can take a deep breath now and rest. Yes, there's been a change! Oh, there's been a change, and the change is *in us*. The wind shift we sense taking place, coming out of this doldrum, is in us. A new fragrance is in the air. It's the sweet aroma of our new trust in Him.

Now you feel your vessel begin to accelerate. You're off and running before the Wind. Well mate, it's time to set a new course heading. Steady as you go!

My dear, dear friends! I love you so much. I do want the very best for you. You make me feel such joy, fill me with such pride. Don't waver. Stay on track, steady in God.
Phil. 4:1, MSG

Spiritual Doldrums

Chapter 9

Winds of Many Doctrines

*Check the horizon and see how different these seas and waves appear. "White caps" are everywhere with a definite **confusion** in the "set of the waves." There's no pattern of movement in these types of waves and no harmony in their flowing. "What's propelling these waves? What kind of wind is it that moves these seas?" you question. Keep your sails set and your focus on Me. I am with you! You may wonder, "How can my vessel pass through these seas with such confusion? The winds must be contrary."*

Vessels can get confused in these waters and lose their direction. Some may want to turn "astern" to go back. But, I say again, keep all your focus on Me. Trust Me to be your compass and to provide you with the wind that will carry you through. You see, on the other side of these waters begins a different sea. It's one of maturity.

Winds of Many Doctrines

*But you must pass through these waters of confused seas that are churned up by **undirected winds**. You see, my son [my daughter], these seas are driven by the "Winds of Many Doctrines."*

Their purpose is to deceive vessels as they are tossed "to and fro," but not if you're focused on me. So stay focused on Me and do not let your heart fear. Waves will come against you on one side and then again on the other side. Although the ride is uncomfortable as waves break over the sides, do not be afraid. Instead, take time to spend with me and know I will provide you with the Winds of My Spirit which will carry you through. I cannot say it enough, stay focused, stay focused, stay focused on Me! I have already walked on these waters and I know what's on the other side of these seas. I will bring you through to new waters and to a new place. Trust Me! I will do what I said I would do.

There are many wonderful things I have for you on the other side, things I cannot tell you quite yet. Just know I am bringing you into a new and safe harbor, one you have never seen before, the "Harbor Of Rest and Refreshing."

Jesus at the Helm

Passage of Persecutions

During a voyage through the Caribbean, I set sail from the British Virgin Islands for St. Martin, a northern island in the string of The Lesser Antilles. There was no other logical course heading except to cross the Anegada Passage. This passage got its name from a nearby Spanish island, meaning "drowned Island." The island is protected by a famous 18 mile long Horse Shoe Reef, one of the worlds largest coral reefs. Anegada Island was once famous as a pirate's hideout, with legends of treasure. However, it is now noted for conch shells and its graveyard of shipwrecks claimed by its dangerous coral reefs.

The Anegada Passage is known for unobstructed rolling swells and frothing breakers of the Atlantic coming down to meet head on with the warm waters of the Caribbean which have a strong westerly current. Mix this in with the prevailing easterly winds and you have the challenging mixture of waters within the Anegada Passage. This is a combination that will put a knot in the stomach of any seasoned sailor. The passage is often considered the "Cape Horn" of the Caribbean. It also has a reputation for vessels encountering hard pounding "square waves" in crossing it. I have to admit I had never heard of "square waves" and wondered what in the world these kind of waves could possibly be like.

Well, I set sail and by evening I was in the Anegada Passage. The wind began singing through the rigging wires, and the bow of my boat was reacting as if it was hitting deep ruts or potholes in a road. A wave would hit my bow with a loud pounding sound and the boat would suddenly jerk to one side. Then another wave would hit on the other side of my bow and pound it to the opposite direction. There was no pattern or set to these waves, no harmony or flow. Then I began to realize that these waves were beginning to form an odd, square shape. Yah mate, these were those square waves I had heard about and they were nothing like I had ever seen before. They slammed into the hull of my vessel with such force it "shivered her timbers," covering my boat with salt spray. This was not at all like the rolling seas I had come to enjoy. Squinting, looking through the dark across the deck of my boat, all I could see was a maze of white capped seas dancing on the horizon. Most puzzling was how these waves seemingly hit both sides of my bow at the same time. Was it from the force of undirected winds that churned up all these waves or was it some kind of weird underlying current? It concerned me more than a little.

I believe that in the spiritual realm all of us, at some time or another, will come to the passage I call "Winds of Many Doctrines." This is a place where the voices of diverse teachings bring confusion into our spiritual journey. Waves of "legalism" come at our vessel from one direction, seas of "religion" from another. The pulling of an undercurrent from the "traditions of men," mixed with the surf of "self-effort" and white capped breakers from condemnation of the "law." Together, it feels like we are being carried about by "seas of strange doctrines," with no harmony or flow.

That's when our hearts need to be established in Grace to stay on course and to complete this crossing. If our focus is *on the seas*, rather than *on Jesus,* it'll be easy to become confused and lose our direction in these "Seas of Disorder."

Winds of Many Doctrines

The Cure for Confusion

*Be not carried about with divers and **strange doctrines**. For it is a good thing that the **heart** be **established** with **Grace**.*

Heb. 13:9, KJV [emphasis mine]

Peter, walking on the water, began to sink when he focused on the sound and confusion of the seas. But when he cried out, Jesus lifted him out of the seas. Many vessels in these confused waters may turn to go back because their *focus* is on the *elements* and *conditions* around them. I say this with a humble sigh, as I have visited this passage more than once in the spiritual realm before making the crossing.

Let's depend on the Holy Spirit to keep our focus on His Grace and we'll make this a successful crossing. Awaiting our arrival on the other side of this passage is a new maturity in our spiritual life.

*So then, we may no longer be children, tossed [like ships] to and fro between chance gusts of teaching and wavering with every changing **Wind of Doctrine**...*

Eph. 4:14, AMP [emphasis mine]

Jesus at the Helm

Doctrines affect our believing. Deceptive doctrines of the enemy can toss us about, like the "religious doctrine" that our own good works gets us to the finish line of our journey. These doctrines are meant to get our eyes off Jesus and on self which result in a course headed for the old port of "Perfection by Self-Effort." That thinking will get us turned around or even lost in these seas. Paul warned the Galatians of the crazy doctrine they were drawn into. They were trying to *finish* a journey by self-effort which they had *begun* in the Spirit.

For only crazy people would think they could complete by their own efforts what was begun by God. If you weren't smart enough or strong enough to begin it, how do you suppose you could perfect it?
Gal. 3:3, MSG

Crossing this passage in the spiritual realm is challenging because the mixture of elements produces the uncanny seas of confusion. Confusion comes from mixture. Spiritually it's a "toxic tonic" parallel to mixing the works of the law with the Grace Gospel. Paul made it clear that *mixing* the two not only brings confusion, but will dilute them both so they loose their power.

And if by grace, then it is no longer of works; otherwise grace is no longer grace. But if it is of works, it is no longer grace; otherwise work is no longer work.

Rom. 11:6, NKJ

The Simplicity of Grace

The point is that grace is not grace if our works play any part in it. The bible calls it *dead works*. You cannot put New Covenant Wine into Old Covenant wine skins. The old vessels will burst, spilling the wine on the ground and the vessels will perish. New Covenant Wine is put into New Covenant Vessels and then both are preserved. We are New Covenant Vessels made to contain the New Covenant Wine or the Grace Gospel which is really the only Gospel. Grace is the person of Jesus.

*For the law was given by Moses, but **grace and truth** came by Jesus Christ.*

John 1:17, KJV [emphasis mine]

The law was sent by Moses, but when Jesus arrived, grace and truth arrived *in Him*. There's been much confusion about the Grace Gospel. Religious people and legalists say that although we were saved by Grace, the rest of our voyage depends upon our *self-effort* and our *performance* of rules to please God. However, Jesus said it's so simple that a child can enter into this New Kingdom.

> *So come on, let's leave the preschool finger painting exercises on Christ and get on with the grand work of art. Grow up in Christ. The basic foundational truths are in place: turning your back on "salvation by self-help" and turning in trust toward God... But there's so much more. Let's get on with it!*
>
> Heb. 6:1-3; MSG

Let me "heave to" for a moment to say what the Grace Gospel is *not*. It is not to be saved by Grace so that we can then use the power of the Holy Spirit to follow a bunch of rules or man made doctrines so that we can finish our journey. It is the finished work of the Cross and the resurrection of Christ, from beginning to end. Let me suggest that as you read the New Testament, replace the word "Grace" with "Jesus" and see how it fits. Jesus is Grace and He is the Gospel or the "Good News." Grace, the unearned, undeserved, unmerited favor of God, reveals the divine influence or power of God in our heart. Peter called it the "manifold grace" or the "many faceted" Grace of God. Like a diamond with many facets, any way you look at Jesus [the Diamond],

His light shines through to create a different beauty from each direction that we see His face. When we look through eyes that are not clouded by law mentality, we will see the Glory of the Lord as in a mirror, then we are changed into His image by the Spirit.

> *But we all, with unveiled face, beholding as in a mirror the glory of the Lord, are being transformed into the same image from glory to glory, just as from the Lord, the Spirit.*
>
> 2 Cor. 3:18, NAS

An "unveiled face" is one that is not covered by a veil of "the law" but is cleared away by "grace" to be able to see the Glory of the Lord. So when we turn to look at Him, we can see His marvelous Grace and His light shining through onto any situation to bring us to the answer we need, no matter how big the problem. It's the love of Jesus and what He has accomplished for us through the cross that is revealed in the Grace Gospel. Through the cross we have been made the *righteousness of God*.

In Hebrews 8, God said He would put His laws in our minds and write them on our hearts. These are *not* the mosaic laws nor the ten commandments. They are the New Covenant laws of love, freedom and liberty. John put it this way: this is the *commandment*, that we should *believe* on the name of Jesus Christ, and to *love* one another. First we believe, then receive His love, and then we can love others.

I'm saying all this to say, it is imperative that we understand how our Father works through our hearts in the New Covenant. When we *think right,* we will *believe right.* When we *believe right*, then we will *live right.*

> *For as he thinks in his heart, so is he.*
> Prov. 23:7, NKJ

A New Confidence

A new intuitive confidence towards God takes place in our hearts when we know we are *right* with Him, that we're complete in Christ, and can do all things through Him. We're fully equipped and gifted to make any crossing the Lord leads us to make. A new growth takes place in us effortlessly during this crossing, as more of the mystery is unveiled inside us.

> *The mystery in a nutshell is just this: Christ is in you, so therefore you can look forward to sharing in God's glory. It's that simple.*
> Col. 1:27, MSG

Because we are in Him, His Glory is being revealed in us by *His* power flowing through us! Not by *our* power. This intrepid confidence we have in Jesus brings a reward of peace and protection, knowing He *will take us over, not under*. We have a Captain who will *not* take us part of the way to leave us there. He will get us safely to the appointed destination no matter what the condition of the seas.

> *Do not, therefore, fling away your fearless* **confidence**, *for it carries a great and glorious compensation of reward.*
> Heb. 10:35, AMP [emphasis mine]

Leave a Trail of Light

In the natural, I noticed something very unusual about the waters in this passage. It must have contained a lot of phosphorus because my rudder left a swirling trail of light in the water for about 100 yards. I don't know how to describe this phenomena except it looks like a trail of millions of little stars in the sky, only they are swirling in the water. As the water is disturbed by any object moving through the sea, the phosphorus is stirred up and leaves a brightly lit trail. I've seen this many times before, but the trail was only a few feet long, not at all like this trail of light.

Jesus at the Helm

So, in the middle of the night I made my way to the bow of the boat to check the tackle, lashed to the deck. With all the pounding, I wanted to make sure everything was secure. I was hanging on for dear life to the hand rails and life lines when I looked off to the port beam and saw a huge trail of light. No, it was two trails of light in the water, headed for my bow at a high speed. It looked like two torpedoes on target for my bow. Now, some time previous to this, I had seen a submarine surface in Caribbean waters just ahead of my boat, moving quite fast, which then dove back under. So I knew subs could be in the area. That brought no peace to my thinking in this situation. The thought hit me, "Was this an accidental discharge of torpedoes? No, it can't be!" Yet here they were, two large objects, lit up and surging through the water, not wavering up or down, left or right. They were straight as a bullet, right on target for my bow. I knew I'd never get to my rigging in time to drop the sails. With only seconds to go, I thought maybe they would pass underneath the hull. I grabbed hold of the lines to prepare for impact. "Maybe they'll just punch a hole in the hull and I'll live to hang on to the floating pieces." I closed my eyes and held my breath.

A large wave of water washed across my bow. And to my astonishment, they made an unbelievable, instant 90 degree turn and broke the surface with a loud blow of air [and it wasn't me gasping for breath]. It was two large [emphasis on large] dolphins wanting to play in the middle of the night by pushing off my bow wave. I took a deep breath. I've seen them hundreds of times before playing off a bow wave, but never like this, flying straight at me on super speed, creating a long stream of light.

As I am reflecting back remembering this incident, I am reminded of the trail of light that my boat was leaving behind as I was knifing through those rough seas. It's a picture of believers in this world sailing through rough times on this life's journey and leaving a trail of light behind. We should be leaving a trail of light, stirred by the love of Jesus, so that others in this world will look with wonder and know that the supernatural love of God has just touched them as we are passing by.

For you were once darkness, but now you are light in the Lord. Walk as children of light.
Eph. 5:8, NKJ

The winds of many doctrines are meant to promote fear, doubt, and confusion in order to get our attention on ourselves and off Jesus, to focus on our *condition* instead of our *position* in Christ, to make us feel alienated from God and wonder if He's really for us or against us. These winds can punch a hole in the hull of our confidence in Him.

Jesus at the Helm

There are two lesser pirates, Fear and Doubt, who will use any opportunity of us wavering to make their way on board our vessel. They bring fear of the sea worthiness of our vessel and doubt as to whether we can successfully stay the course and cross this difficult passage. Paul admonishes us to stand firm against the schemes of the devil. The enemy knows that on the other side of this spiritual passage, we will no longer be children tossed about by every *wave of doctrine*. Doubt, fear and confusion are his tactics to get us to turn astern, to go back searching for the overcrowded "Port of Indecision."

Nevertheless, we can stand firm in Christ, confident that He has made us a seaworthy vessel. He made us worthy at the Cross. And He made us well able to cross any passage. We've been given a reliable Navigator, who is ever inside and at our side to teach us, to comfort us, and to encourage us. Regardless of any seas that may be tossing our vessel to and fro, trust Him to keep us on course and make our crossing successful.

Grace is a loving, kind teacher even when we go through hard times. Love is a greater motivator than fear. Let's give our hearts over to Grace and we will not back off from what we believe. The pirates, Fear and Doubt, will no longer have a place on board. Their demise will be at the end of a gangplank. Peace and Confidence will become our new companions. With our hearts and minds stable and secure, the favor of God surrounds us and brings us into greater things that lie ahead. It is our destiny, our calling, and it's sure. New doors of opportunities will be opened for us to be an influence to others.

Landfall, Rest, Refreshing

When Jesus says, "Let us cross over to the other side," then hang on to the "gunwales" because we're going safely to the other side of this passage.

I know what I'm doing. I have it all planned out – plans to take care of you, not abandon you, plans to give you the future you hope for.
Jer. 29:11, MSG

The morning daylight broke through on the horizon and I was squinting to see any landfall that would confirm I had crossed the Anegada Passage. Yes, I could see it looking through my binocs. St. Martin was a small bump on the horizon. I turned to look back off the stern of my vessel and I could still see the white capped, confused seas, bubbling and frothing on the surface though now it was beginning to fade off into the distance.

It wasn't long before I could see the beautiful green hills of St. Martin. Nestled into the back drop of those green hills was a small port with a number of sailing vessels sitting comfortably on anchor, resting calm and safe. Yes, I did it. I had crossed the Anegada Passage!

Fatigued from little to no sleep and feeling a bit battered, there was a new sense of victory and excitement as I was entering this new port. Crossing the Anegada Passage had made an impact in my sailing life. It was an experience that had answered some questions for me that could not have come any other way. It gave me a confidence in the seaworthiness of my vessel. I knew it was able to withstand the hard pounding seas of this passage. I also had a new sense of accomplishment, knowing that I could navigate through the confused waters of this passage and stay on course.

I maneuvered my boat around in the anchorage to a protected place and dropped anchor. Enjoying a calm rest in the Caribbean breeze, I reflected back on the experience that laid behind me and anticipated the adventures that lay ahead of me.

In the spiritual realm, I believe when we cross this passage, Winds of Many Doctrines, we will begin to feel a weight lifted off our shoulders. In its place we will feel a *yoke of ease*. He is bringing us into a beautiful place of anchorage nestled against the lush green hills of God's rest. He is bringing us to a new and safe harbor, a harbor of refuge where the hills of peace and safety surround us. We are no longer under cunning, crafty doctrines of men that bring bondage and heavy yokes. Oh, the simplicity of Christ, the depth of His love cannot be measured.

For even if the mountains walk away and the hills fall to pieces, My love won't walk away from you, my covenant commitment of peace won't fall apart...
Is. 54:10, MSG

This is a new and different kind of place, one that we've never visited in the past. This will be our new "hailing port" from which we will sail to all other destinations. This is the "Harbor of Rest and Refreshing."

...being confident of this very thing, that He who has begun a good work in you will complete it until the day of Jesus Christ.
Eph. 1:6, NKJ

The Captain of our salvation has brought a new confidence into our journey. The Greek meaning for "salvation" [sozo] is "prosperous, healed, whole, well, safe, delivered, protected, and preserved." These are our promises provided and revealed through the Cross.

We are now on our "destiny time line," laid out by our Abba Father. We are setting sail on a course heading with a new kind of victory and success under our belt. Having crossed this spiritual passage, we see a new

Jesus at the Helm

maturity has taken place. It's given us a brand new vision accompanied by a new boldness and courage. Now we can sail our predestined course through the deep blue waters of Grace, with a new and permanent inner rest. We are seeing our first love in a clearer focus now!

Saving is all his idea, and all his work. All we do is trust him enough to let him do it. It's God's gift from start to finish!
Eph. 2:8, MSG

Winds of Many Doctrines

Chapter 10

Setting Your Course

You have all the equipment you need with which to set your course and stay on course. I have placed them in you. But before you set your course, what is your destination? What is your plan? Is it My plan and My destination or is it yours? Take time to spend with Me and to find out My plan for your life. Don't ask me to just bless your plan on your destination.

My son [daughter], I have many promises for you that are still waiting to be fulfilled in you, but you need to be prepared to receive them. I am preparing you, bringing to maturity the gifts and skills in your life. Are you ready? Let us take them together as I have set them before you. You will see these promises manifest in you, while you are under sail and entering "ports," even "foreign ports" that you have never seen before.

Setting Your Course

Each port that you enter will require different skills to avoid the dangers of reefs, shoals, currents, rocks, waves, and shallows. So don't be in a hurry. Let's get My plan and set our course together. Then you will be able to acknowledge Me on your course headings, en route to your destinations. This will be your confidence when any difficulties should come and when the enemy tries to move you off course. You can confidently say, "My God has shown me this course. I will not fear! He is the one I acknowledge and He directs my course!"

Jesus at the Helm

Check Your Charts

Before I set sail for any long journey I would *study* my charts and not just casually look at them. I have reckoned my charts to be like my bible. Charts reveal the direction of *"true north"* and other details of the ocean: depths, currents, reefs, shoals, islands, latitude/longitude and much more. Charts, like bible scriptures, contain valuable information if you understand them correctly. If you lack understanding in how to read charts then you'll need someone to help you or they can be misleading.

The same is true of bible scriptures. They will reveal the *"true Jesus,"* if we understand them. If not, they could mislead us and misrepresent Jesus. Scriptures are "God breathed," by inspiration of the Holy Spirit and need to be read by inspiration of the Holy Spirit, our Helper!

But the natural man does not receive the things of the Spirit of God... because they are spiritually discerned.
                                        1 Cor. 2:14, NKJ

He gives us an understanding of the scriptures so that they become the "Word of God," seen through God's eyes and not through the eyes of the natural man. If we read scriptures through a law or religious mentality, we'll get a distorted view of God's love and Who He is. That, my friend, can cause us big problems. I've been there and it caused me many years of pain and deception. However, when we read scriptures through a Grace mentality we will receive the revelation of scriptures from God's perspective, the "True Gospel."

On all charts, there's printed a "compass rose" that gives a picture of true north. It helps you to find an accurate "compass course" heading. In the Word of God, there is also a "true north," *Jesus*, who is the **true focal point**. The Holy Spirit reveals Jesus to us in the Word, and that keeps us on our spiritual course heading, to arrive at the right place at the right time. When we understand that the "Gospel," *is* the finished work of Jesus through the Cross, our perception will change. We'll see everything through the new eyes of Grace. We will read our "spiritual charts" [bible] differently. The Gospel will open up new treasures to us that have been veiled by the law or religion.

Sail His Plan

When I would lay out my course heading, I would plot a rhumb [straight] line to my port or destination. However, I had to to make course adjustments for reefs, currents, wind, etc. For a sailing vessel, just a wind shift could mean a course change. If a storm came up, you had to learn how to deal with it. You don't outrun a storm in a sailboat.

It's similar in the spiritual realm. Storms will come, but the Holy Spirit will help us make it through them. We've been given spiritual gifts and skills that we learn to use as we are under sail on our journey. It's "OJT" [On the Job Training]. So, let's not be in a hurry. Our Navigator, the Holy Spirit, will be our teacher and will show us God's compass course to our destination. Let's follow His plan.

"For I know the plans I have for you," says the Lord. "They are plans for good and not for disaster, to give you a future and a hope."

Jer. 29:11, NLT

Let the Holy Spirit bring understanding for our spiritual charts [bible] and we'll receive revelations that bypass our reasoning minds. He will show us where and when it's time to set sail and we will avoid possible wrong influences of people with wrong motives. In other words, we'll learn to follow the Spirit and not the crowd. However, always be willing to make any course adjustments of the Spirit. We may think His course doesn't look like the best route, but He knows and recognizes any dangers ahead in the water. He knows the true course that will bring us through the precarious

Setting Your Course

waters to our destination.

...He will guide you into all truth...

John 16:13, KJV

I was sailing off the coast of the Dominican Republic when a storm spawned two "water spouts" off my port bow. I started to change course to "starboard," but a pod of whales with a calf were "breaching" on my starboard. Caught between whales and water spouts, it "shivered my timbers." It's a bad mistake, mate, to ever get your vessel between a cow and her calf. Your vessel could end up in splinters.

I dropped my sails down to the size of a handkerchief and waited for the circumstances to change before I could change course. I sure didn't feel I was at the right place at the right time and would have preferred to have been any place other than there. By the grace of God I was able to slide between the whales and water spouts. Even though I was running from God, He still protected me.

When we fully understand how we have been sealed with the Holy Spirit as our Navigator, it will change our whole life. We'll be able to rest and enjoy the trip, knowing that He will bring us through the storms of discouragement, currents of deception, and waves of adversity. He guides us around shoals of depression, rocks of debt, bypassing the hard, harsh words of criticism and rejection. He threads us through the narrow passes lined with rocks and boulders of the law on one side with jagged coral reefs of religion on the other side. As you know, the devil's plan is to divert our focus and run us aground, but the Holy Spirit has a different plan, one that was created at the foundation of the world.

> *For we are God's [own] handiwork... recreated in Christ Jesus, [born anew] that we may do those good works which God predestined [planned beforehand] for us [taking paths which He prepared ahead of time]... [**living the good life** which He prearranged...]*
> Eph. 2:10, AMP [emphasis mine]

God has many promises and surprises ahead for us on this journey and they are all "yes and amen" in Jesus. Maybe it surprises you that He sees us as victorious overcomers in this life. When our sails are set on His course, we will arrive at our appointed destination amazed at what He did *in us*.

Led, Not Driven

When it comes to learning about setting our course, we need to look to Jesus who always knew His course and His destination. His most radical destination, of course, was the Cross, but He was led to many other destinations before the Cross. He never got lost and He never wavered off His Love course. How was it that Jesus always knew His course headings? When Jesus was baptized in the Jordan river, the heavens opened and the Spirit of God descended upon Him like a dove. A voice from heaven declared, "this is My Son, in Him I'm well pleased." He was immediately *led of the Spirit* into the wilderness to be tempted. The Holy Spirit revealed to Jesus His course heading, His destination and His trials ahead. Remember, Jesus did not perform any miracles until after He was baptized and led of the Holy Spirit. Later, we would hear Jesus often saying; "I only do what I see My Father doing!" He saw into the spiritual realm the same way we can see, by the Holy Spirit. We're sailing this course empowered the same way as Jesus. If Jesus received His destinations and course headings from the Holy Spirit, why should it be any different for us?

For as many as are led by the Spirit of God, they are the sons of God.

Rom. 8:14, KJV

The good news is that, as sons of God, our Abba Father has equipped us and laid out a course planned ahead for us. We are *living epistles* learning to flow with the Wind of the Holy Spirit on this exciting journey in our life. We have been commissioned by the Lord, as seafaring men and women, to live a life radically different from that of a "landlubber" [person unfamiliar with sailing]. We are no longer hanging around the fringes of ocean waters, dreaming of voyages to the unknown and never setting sail. We are, instead, hoisting sails for the deep blue spiritual waters to destinations and ports determined by the Lord. A Christian life should be a radically different life of excitement, one that is led into adventures of amazement and fun. When we are *led*, we are flowing in *His strength*, not ours.

> *[Not in your own strength] for it is God Who is all the while effectually at work in you [energizing and creating in you the power and desire], both to will and to work for His good pleasure and satisfaction and delight.*
>
> Phil. 2:13, AMP

Jesus works in our hearts where He places desires and destinations. As we delight ourselves in Him, we will sense our course headings by the Holy Spirit. He teaches us how to be sensitive to the spiritual realm and leads us into divine connections where we will share the love of Jesus as His ambassadors. People will see the reflection of Jesus and His Glory in us.

People flocked from all over to sit at the feet of Jesus and listen. Why? Because they felt so loved, so accepted, and so comfortable around Him. Even so,

Setting Your Course

Jesus never condoned sin or destructive life styles. Instead, He taught a radical message of love and acceptance. He demonstrated the heart of the Father and drew people to Himself with non-condemning words of love. His "navigation" was always perfect. He was consistently at the right place at the right time. He went where people were in order to minister the love of God. That's our Captain, the One on board with us.

Keep your eyes on Jesus, who both began and finished this race we're in. Study how he did it. Because he never lost sight of where he was headed...
Heb. 12:2, MSG

Yet, it must have appeared to the disciples, at times, that Jesus had veered off course, like going out of His way to meet a woman at a well in Samaria. She had no idea that the Creator of Living Waters had come to meet her at the well. That encounter changed the course of her life forever, and not hers only, but a whole town experienced revival!

Driven, Not Led

Our enemy tries to get us focused on any ambitious plans that will veer us off course to miss our "divine connections." We have been set free from our own self reliant plans. They will always fall short of the glory of God, leaving us to flounder in our religious projects. Self reliance, my friend, will always drive us off course. We may not even realize our course heading has changed, until we feel out of breath, out of rest, and out of Grace.

> *I suspect you would never intend this, but this is what happens. When you attempt to live by your own religious plans and projects, you are cut off from Christ, you fall out of grace.*
> Gal. 5:4, MSG

Have you ever dealt with sea sickness? In the natural, it's a very nasty feeling. It's a *motion problem.* Your brain is not in sync or rhythm with the seas. The cure is to stop looking at your vessel and the waves. Instead, focus on the horizon which is always *consistent and stable.*

The same is true with a "spiritual sea sickness." Have you ever been following your own plan and just knew you were on the wrong course heading? It's an ugly feeling that hits you in the pit of your stomach. Somewhere you got off course, got under the law and began to focus on what you must do. It's a motion problem. You know you're not in sync or rhythm with the Grace course heading that God had put you on. The cure is the same for that spiritual yuck feeling as it is in

Setting Your Course

the natural. Change your focus from being on your vessel, your circumstances and your "to do" list, and put it back onto Jesus. He is the *always consistent and stable One.* That spiritual yuck feeling will begin to leave and the Spirit will get you back on course.

Focused on Jesus, the bright and morning star, we are *led, not driven.* Paul warned of the danger of coming back under a "yoke of slavery," by returning to "law mentality."

> *You have been severed from Christ, you who are seeking to be justified by law; you have **fallen** from grace.*
>
> Gal. 5:4, NAS [emphasis mine]

The word "fallen" here, in the Greek, means "to be driven off course." Being "severed from Christ" does not mean we lose our salvation. It means we have taken control of our vessel to sail our own course, using our own plan. You cannot sail in grace and law at the same time. They are opposite mindsets. The law plan makes you a slave to rules, and condemnation will surely follow. The Grace plan makes us free to follow the Spirit of the Lord where there is liberty, and peace will automatically follow.

Operating in the law plan is like putting a magnet next to a compass. The needle jumps around and you can no longer find true north. The same is true with our spiritual internal compass when we get back under the law. The needle jumps around, we get confused and out of harmony and peace, losing our true north [Jesus] direction. We can then be driven off course into shallow waters of the flesh and dangerous reefs of religion. If your inner peace is disturbed, check your internal compass to see if you have let your vessel be driven onto a law-minded course.

> *And let the peace [soul harmony which comes] from Christ rule [act as **umpire** continually] in your hearts [deciding and settling with finality all questions that arise in your minds...]*
>
> Col. 3:15, AMP [emphasis mine]

If you've veered off course, just ask the Holy Spirit to help you refocus. It takes the power of the Holy Spirit to help get our focus and internal compass back on true north, [Jesus]. As we do, everything outside will grow strangely dim and we will regain that harmony of flowing again. The Holy Spirit can supernaturally get us back on course. You may hear Him say, "Recalculating!" Just remember, we are *living* epistles not *doing* epistles.

Setting Your Course

Pursuit of a Star

Everywhere you look you can see Jesus. The wise men came out of the east to find the King of the Jews, saying, "We have seen His star." That star led them to Jesus.

When the sailors of old made long ocean voyages, they kept their vision on the North Star or Polaris, during the night time. One of the brightest stars in our sky by far is found off the lip of the big dipper. A plumb line dropped from the North Star to the horizon would be almost exact true north. Sailors used the North Star because it was *stable* and *accurate* in it's position. The Star that never changes, is the same yesterday, today, and forever, is Jesus!

> *Keep your eyes on Jesus, who both began and finished this race we're in. Study how he did it. Because he never lost sight of where he was headed – that exhilarating finish in and with God – he could put up with anything along the way: cross, shame, whatever.*
>
> Heb. 12:2, MSG

When dawn comes and the bright and morning star pushes back all the darkness, the daylight comes streaming in. The book of Revelations refers to Jesus as the bright and morning star. I can tell you that there are few sights as awesome and as beautiful as the bright and morning sun coming up on the horizon of the ocean while you are under sail and far off shore.

...until the day dawn, and the day star arise in your hearts.

2 Pet. 1:19, KJV

What an awesome picture of our wonderful savior coming up in our hearts as the bright and shining light after sailing through the dark of night. The Holy Spirit is always there to point us to the *Star* that leads us to our Ports of Destination, even Foreign Ports we've never thought or dreamed possible.

Local Knowledge

Let me drop anchor here for a moment and share an old Salt's story of sailing into Puerto Plata of the Dominican Republic. At the time it was a very tricky port to sail into. You wouldn't want to try it at night with reefs and other obstacles close by at the entry.

I was approaching Puerto Plata several miles offshore in the dark and noticed the lights of a number of vessels lined up for a distance, waiting for daybreak to enter the port. Upon entering and dropping anchor, I noticed one

Setting Your Course

of the vessels that came in. It was a large Coast Guard vessel. Some friends of mine were invited to tour the vessel and they later shared a funny story. Awed by the ship's large navigation room with all the latest equipment, they found it humorous that a certain book was located right in front of the helm. It was a book used by most cruising sailors in the Caribbean during those years. Written by a sailor that had traveled to most of the ports in the Caribbean, it was a wealth of information containing hand drawn diagrams of how to safely enter Caribbean ports. The diagrams were birthed out of the author's personal knowledge, or in sailors terms, "local knowledge" of port entries. His drawings would show how to navigate around dangerous shoals, reefs, and wreckages. For example, his drawing would line up a conspicuous house on a hill with some other land mark to give a visual sighting of how to enter the port safely.

The humor to the story is that the helmsman of the Coast Guard boat, with all the "high tech" navigational equipment on board, preferred to use the hand drawn pictures in the book in order to enter Puerta Plata. There's nothing wrong with high tech equipment, but often "local knowledge" drawings by someone who has been there feels more trustworthy.

The point I want to make is that we have a spiritual Navigator with more local knowledge than we could ever need. He's already *visited* our tomorrow. Nothing is more high tech than our Comforter who brings us into and out of precarious problems and tight places with ease.

By your words I can see where I'm going; they throw a beam of light on my dark path.
Ps. 119:105, MSG

Our Comforter

The Holy Spirit fine tunes the gifts and skills placed in us. If life's cares close in and we feel weak, He encourages us by reminding us *whose* vessel we are. He makes our voyages successful even if they seem impossible. He gets us to where we're going with *joy*. If need be, He will draw us a picture or a diagram that reveals a state of no fret, no worry, no stress. Just Be Happy!

We are brand new created vessels whom Jesus made the "righteousness of God" to confirm His plan and calling on our lives. He has placed us in the secret place of life and safety.

In the way of righteousness is life, and in it's pathway there is no death.
Prov. 12:28, NKJ

Setting Your Course

It was by Grace through trusting Jesus that we've received the *gift* of righteousness, not by our *works* otherwise we could *boast* [Eph. 2:8-9]. If our efforts can't make us right with God, then our efforts can't make us wrong with God.

Trust God from the bottom of your heart; don't try to figure out everything on your own. Listen for God's voice in everything you do, everywhere you go; He's the one who will keep you on track [course].
Prov. 3:5-6, MSG [additional word mine]

Therefore, we can stop trying to figure out everything on this journey and just be who we're made to be. *Understanding* is not a port we arrive at. It comes *during* our voyage. Salvation is a journey not a destination. What's our part? It's just simple *trust* in Him from our heart that casts out fear so we can *rest*. In the Noah Webster dictionary, "trust" is defined as "a reliance or *resting* of the mind on the *integrity*, veracity, justice, friendship or other sound principle of another person."

As vessels traveling in this new way of Grace, we can rest our minds and confidently trust in the integrity of Jesus. His peace and exceeding promises manifest in our lives effortlessly during our voyage. He brings refreshing so we can enjoy the journey.

Jesus at the Helm

We may unknowingly sail out of the waters of fear and into the waters of blessing and favor which are supernaturally located on our course heading. That's when we will recognize that we have left those shallow waters of envy and jealousy that used to manifest when we saw others blessed. Why? Because we know that we are the beloved of the Lord and that the favor of God resides in us and on us.

> *That means we will not compare ourselves with each other as if one of us were better and another worse. We have far more interesting things to do with our lives. Each of us is an **original**.*
> Gal. 5:26, MSG [emphasis mine]

We can trust in Him not to just get us to our destination but more importantly to our DESTINY. We are trophies of His Grace. Jesus takes ordinary vessels and does extraordinary things with them. It's all been planned, appointed, and destined by our Daddy.

Count on it! Rely on it! It's our inheritance!

Setting Your Course

Chapter 11

Sailing In Our Inheritance

*You can tell for sure that you are now fully adopted as his own children because God sent the Spirit of his Son into our lives crying out, "Papa! Father!" Doesn't that privilege of intimate conversation with God make it plain that you are not a slave, but a child? And if you are a child, you're also an heir, with complete access to the **inheritance**.*

Gal. 4:6-7, MSG [emphasis mine]

We've been talking about sailing out our destiny all through this book though not by our own efforts or works, nor by our own wisdom and understanding. Through the finished work of the cross and resurrection of Jesus, it's all been purchased for us. And by the Holy Spirit, it's been placed inside us.

Sailing In Our Inheritance

This chapter, however, is a little different from the previous ones. Rather than begin with a word of knowledge, I would like for us to sail into an area precious to our Lord on this journey. As His children, we have an inheritance in God. I believe we may have missed the significance of this awesome promise and failed to rely on it, or as He said to me, "Count on it!" It's been purchased for every child of God, it's our *inheritance*.

Jesus died on the cross to bring His last will and new testament or covenant, into effect. He was raised from the dead to enforce this new covenant that He purchased for all believers, with all its provisions and promises. Our part is just to believe it, then rest in it.

An inheritance through a will and testament is not based on performance but on *relationship* or *kinship*. If we try to finish, by our own efforts, what Jesus has already finished, we will end up in unbelief. Let's just accept our inheritance, not because it is given based on our actions, but understanding that we are *qualified* simply because we are His *children,* in His family.

*Like a will that takes effect when someone dies, the new covenant was put into action at Jesus' death. His death marked the transition from the old plan to the new one, canceling the old obligations and accompanying sins, and summoning the **heirs** to receive the eternal **inheritance** that was promised them...*

Heb. 9:16-17, MSG [emphasis mine]

Humble Inheritance

Many believers think it's not humble to say that God's gifts and promises belong to us just because we are His children. Often, they will insinuate that we have to earn it. No one is perfect enough to earn it, but our righteousness, through Jesus, has *qualified* us to *receive* it. Our inheritance, as children, was sealed forever through His resurrection.

One day as I was walking and just talking with the Lord about some needs and concerns, He reminded me, "Son, you have *My inheritance, count* on it, *rest* in it!"

Well mate, that caught me off guard and got me to feeling real good. I have an inheritance just because I'm His child, not because I'm a perfect Christian. I've anchored that word in my heart and it's better than finding a hidden chest of gold. We are qualified because we are His children.

> *...giving thanks to the Father, who has **qualified** you to share in the **inheritance** of the saints in light.*
> Col. 1:12-14, ESV [emphasis mine]

During the time I spent running from God, I went on a trip to Costa Rica seeking gold. I and another chap managed to get a "sluice box" with a Briggs and Stratton suction pump engine into the back hills of a gold mining peninsula in Costa Rica. First, we spent several days in a small town jail for our stealthy move of sneaking gold mining equipment into the country. We represented ourselves as "geologists" wanting to study rocks and metals found in local rivers. That failed to get us exonerated, but a friend who knew the local authorities came by to visit the police major and put in a good word for us, along with some "paper persuasion." We were released with all our equipment.

It was excellent equipment for gold mining, but obviously we didn't have the expertise. For days we tried all along a river supposedly known for gold. The result left us totally empty handed. How many times have we tried our own method of finding worldly treasures only to come up empty handed, perhaps even broke, busted or disgusted?

However, we have a promise from God that if we'll just seek His righteousness and His kingdom, He will care for us better than we can *ever* care for ourselves. Nevertheless, at that time in my life I just didn't get it.

Let's not get off course, struggling in our own efforts on a course heading for the treasures of the world. Let's instead sail His course and discover His hidden treasures, that are already on board. God wants the *very best* for us and it's all been laid out for us as an inheritance. Let's receive all that belongs to us and expect "over the top" blessings not limited by small thinking. It's our destiny and it's our inheritance.

I know what I'm doing. I have it all planned out – plans to take care of you, not abandon you, plans to give you the future you hope for.
Jer. 29:11, MSG

It was some years later that I realized that God loves His children too much to leave us in the condition He found us. So, He takes us on a sailing journey across an Ocean of Grace to discover *our inheritance*. Our entire sailing journey is all about discovering God's goodness in which His treasures are hidden. He wants us to be adventuresome and bold in His Kingdom and to discover those treasures.

His delight is in us! He is more than cheerful about us, even when we do something wrong. Thankfully, our mistakes do not disqualify us from His promises in our inheritance.

In him we have obtained an inheritance, having been predestined according to the purpose of him who works all things according to the counsel of his will.
Eph. 1:11, ESV

Heart Issues

I believe that God wants to reveal to us three foundational heart issues on this journey. They belong to us and are part of our inheritance. They are His *love*, His *assurance* and His *freedom* through Christ.

Jesus was busy revealing to us the Father's character through His ministry here on earth. Paul spoke of the Father as our Daddy who *loves* us unconditionally. He wants us to rest *assured* in His desire to care for us. And through His love and care, we will find true *freedom*. Freedom from fear. Freedom from doubt. Freedom from our own efforts and performance to earn our own care and desires. He wants us to experience freedom from the world's system of self-reliance and to live out a new life in the spirit realm that lets us *relax* in His love. He wants us to let the Wind of the Spirit move us through the waters of life as God's children in His "Elite Fleet."

We were not just randomly chosen. We were particularly picked to be part of the peculiar family of God in Christ, by which He declared us holy [uncommon, separated] and righteous in His love. We have become emissaries in the Kingdom of God by receiving His *righteousness*, through the Grace of Jesus!

> *...much more will those who receive the abundance of grace and the free gift of righteousness* **reign in life** *through the one man Jesus Christ.*
>
> Rom. 5:17, ESV [emphasis mine]

His Love

How do we sail our journey being convinced and confident that God really *loves* us? The proof is in the pudding, mate. On the Cross, with the arms of Jesus outstretched to us, His awesome love is extended to us.

> *This is the kind of love we are talking about – not that we once upon a time loved God, but that he loved us and sent his Son as a sacrifice to clear away our sins and the damage they've done to our relationship with God.*
>
> 1 John 4:10, MSG

Sailing In Our Inheritance

God didn't wait for us to make a step towards Him. He made the first step towards us! God sent forth His Son, His greatest gift, a sacrifice for our sins and the sins of the world, to those who would believe in Him. As one song says, "His love never fails, it never gives up, and it never runs out on me!" That's His love.

> *Long before he laid down earth's foundations, he had us in mind, had settled on us as the focus of his love, to be made whole and holy by his love. Long, long ago he decided to adopt us into his family through Jesus Christ. [What pleasure he took in planning this!]*
>
> Eph. 1:4-5, MSG

I think that Christians have come to believe that they may have squandered their inheritance and that their future is bleak because of their past. However, Jesus gave us a beautiful picture of our Heavenly Father in relation to our inheritance through the story of the Prodigal Son, who had squandered his inheritance. This son finally came to the end of himself. He sailed into a doldrum with no place else to go. All his inheritance was spent, and being hungry, he decided to return home and ask his father to hire him on as a servant. Before he reached his father's house, being a long way off, his father saw him. He pulled up his robe and ran to meet his son. The Father released the full force of His Grace upon His Son! [Wherever sin abounds, Grace much more abounds.] He fell on his neck, kissed him and embraced him, while the son started his rehearsed speech of being unworthy to be his son and asking forgiveness. It was almost as if the Father was not listening, ordering his servants to quickly bring the best robe and put it on him. He instructed they put a ring on his hand, and shoes on his feet, kill the fattened calf and celebrate! His son, who was dead, had returned to life! He who was lost in self-effort, searching for love and contentment, had now found life in his Father's Grace. His Daddy threw him a *party!* This story reveals the love of our Daddy for us today.

> *...you'll be able to take in with all Christians the **extravagant dimensions** of Christ's love. Reach out and experience the breadth! Test its length! Plumb the depths! Rise to the heights! Live full lives, full in the fullness of God.*
>
> Eph. 3:18-19, MSG [emphasis mine]

No matter what our past, the Father longs to show us His love, to redeem the time, to recover what's been lost and to bring *abundance* back to our lives.

The inheritance we have is not in short supply. In Phil. 4:19, it says that *He supplies all our needs according to His riches in glory, in Christ Jesus!* His riches in glory are not in short supply and therefore our inheritance is bountiful in promises and provisions through trusting Jesus.

In the Prodigal Son story, Jesus reveals to us that our Daddy so totally and passionately loves us that he puts His *best robe* on us. That would be the *robe of righteousness* which Jesus purchased through His finished work on the cross. We are totally in right standing with our Father. Then He said to put a *ring* on His son's finger.

Let me "heave to" here for a moment. I had a dream not long ago. I kept hearing the words, "insignia ring." I've checked out the dictionary several times for the meaning: "an emblem or badge of *honor*; a symbol or token of personal *power*, status, office, or of an official *body* of jurisdiction or general *authority*."

I believe God was revealing that the son's ring represented an insignia ring, placing him, and us, into the *body of Christ,* as part of the family with an *inheritance*. Our Daddy restores *honor* and *authority* to us!

Next the Father said to put sandals or shoes on his feet. Servants or slaves may go barefoot but *children* wear shoes. In Ephesians 6, where it describes the full armor of God, shoes represent the *Gospel of Peace*. Every place we travel on this journey we bring the good news of peace.

Jesus at the Helm

The son was restored and clothed with apparel to help him understand *who he was* within the *family*. Authority has been restored to walk in victory and dominion and as "more than a conqueror" in our never ending inheritance. Our names are in the will, not dependent on our *performance,* nor *disqualified* for our *past mistakes*!

> *It's in Christ that you, once you heard the truth and believed it (this Message of your salvation), found yourselves home free—signed, sealed, and delivered by the Holy Spirit. This **signet** from God is the first installment on what's coming.*
> Eph. 1:13-14, MSG [emphasis mine]

It's always been about our believing in Jesus and trusting Him for our inheritance. Let's just humble ourselves and receive our inheritance. It's His love!

Assurance/Convinced

It's sad when we're not even *aware* of the great and wonderful things that have been placed inside of us, or to know what marvelous promises we have inherited. Thus, we may begin a journey for a vestige of reality, finding only counterfeit answers for what we *already have*.

The Lord's desire is to *assure* our hearts that He will *provide* for us as He has promised. And in that, we can be confident that He will never leave us.

> ...Be relaxed with what you have. Since God **assured** us, "I'll never let you down, never walk off and leave you,"
>
> Heb. 13:5, MSG [emphasis mine]

We can enjoy a biblical hope, the confident expectation of good, embracing with assurance that God holds nothing against us. We are eternally forgiven for all sin – past, present, and future. Our born again spirit man is infused with the Holy Spirit, sanctified and perfected forever. God is not imputing trespasses to us, the slate is wiped clean forever.

> *For by one offering he hath **perfected for ever** them that are **sanctified**... And their **sins** and **iniquities** will I remember no more.*
>
> Heb. 10:14,17; KJV [emphasis mine]

Doesn't that just lift a load off your mind, knowing you are in right standing with our Heavenly Father and nothing can change that? When God cuts a covenant, we can count on it, not by our feelings but by His Word. Often, believers don't *feel* forgiven or loved, so they entertain doubts. *Feelings* are just a mirage on the "Horizon of Doubt."

When we make a contract to purchase a house, we don't question if the house belongs to us based on our feelings, but rather on our contract. Why should we base the reality of a covenant with God on our feelings?

A contract requires that we make payments and when it's fully paid off, we get the deed. It's legally ours, with all the benefits, for the rest of our lives. The same is true of our covenant with God, but with a couple major differences. Jesus made this covenant with our Father, then He made the complete payment for us when He said, "It is finished." Jesus *completed* our part of the covenant for all eternity, if we'll believe it and receive it. A covenant cannot be broken and that is our inheritance.

What if someone told you that your house has been paid off? You would just go to the courthouse and pick up the deed. If you believe in your heart that it's true, you'll go pick up the deed. Then, your heart is *assured* that you own the house. But if you don't believe it, and never pick up the deed, you miss out on owning the house and all the benefits that go with it.

But what's really incomprehensible is if the house has been paid for, the deed already put in your name, and you not only don't claim it, but you just keep sending in payments. Welcome to the law! You just keep paying on what's already been paid for and given to you. You are missing the full benefits of ownership. You work up a hard sweat trying to own what already belongs to you. You keep depleting your account, paying for what you own as a family member with an inheritance.

Why don't you choose to be led by the Spirit and so escape the erratic compulsions of a law-dominated existence?

Gal. 5:18, MSG

If you don't know the truth, the price will go up. You pay for it in condemnation and guilt, not knowing your sins were cleansed at the Cross. You pay for it in fear and worry, not knowing the debt is paid. You pay for it in stress and sickness, not believing the furrows on Jesus back paid for your healing. You'll be working for money instead of money working for you. In your "salvation package," it was all included along with the Holy Spirit to seal the deal. Receive your inheritance in the finished work of Christ!

Let's allow the Holy Spirit to confirm and assure our hearts of our new covenant inheritance. Since Jesus is the "guarantor" of this Covenant, we cannot screw it up! The promises *rest on His shoulders*, not on our performance.

Jesus at the Helm

Conscience/Guilt

I want to take time here to talk about the "conscience." If we don't understand our conscience, I believe it can hinder us from drawing near to God in full assurance. We may end up being more sin conscious than Son conscious. That will produce condemnation. We have to understand our righteousness in this new covenant.

> *For our sake he made him to be sin who knew no sin, so that in him we might become the righteousness of God.*
>
> 2 Cor. 5:21, ESV

We have to distinguish between our conscience and the leading of the Holy Spirit. I don't pretend to know everything about the subject of the conscience, but I can tell you that I suffered a great deal for years because I never had correct teaching about the Holy Spirit. Whenever I felt guilty or condemned, I thought it was the Holy Spirit making me feel that way to correct me. I felt like I was in a pit and with no way out. It was years before I understood that the enemy was using my conscience against me. We have to know that the Holy Spirit *never* uses or corrects us with guilt or condemnation.

Maybe you've heard it said, "Let your conscience be your guide." That's not true for new covenant believers. It's the job of the *Holy Spirit* to lead and guide us. He does that mostly through the Word. He speaks directions and desires to our hearts. If we sin, He reminds us of who we are in Christ, and helps us through our failures or sin. He is not resident in our life to constantly remind us of our sins. That would make us more sin conscious and we would hide in *shame* like Adam and Eve did. He wants us conscious of Jesus and how right we are with our Daddy.

Our conscience can accuse us and bring guilt or it can excuse us. Either one of which could conflict with the leading of the Holy Spirit. The conscience, I believe, has intuitive and learned knowledge. It can operate by laws of right or wrong, or our own rules of right and wrong. In contrast, the Holy Spirit leads us into *life* and out of death. "Right and wrong" are no longer the issues.

*For the law of the **Spirit of life** in Christ Jesus hath made me free from the **law of sin and death**.*
Rom. 8:2, KJV [emphasis mine]

Sailing our journey into what's *life* is the course heading of the *Spirit*. Romans 7:6 says that we serve in the *newness of Spirit*, and not in the oldness of the letter or law. That's the leading of the Holy Spirit and we need to learn to yield to Him. It doesn't mean that we ignore our conscience but if our conscience makes us feel condemned, just know that condemnation is never from God. He will quiet our conscience when it's out of step with His leading.

Let me give you an example. I drove up to a corner where a homeless person was standing with a cardboard sign. My conscience was saying to give money to this guy, but the Holy Spirit interrupted and said, "Don't do it, he is going to use it for alcohol." Now please, I am *not* saying to not give to the homeless. Do whatever the Holy Spirit leads you to do. But what I am saying, is that I had to go through a period in my life when the Holy Spirit weaned me from living by my conscience. I had to let the Holy Spirit deal with my conscience when I felt condemned. I believe He renews our conscience to get in step with the Spirit. It takes time and I believe we often deal with this when we're young in the Lord.

For if our heart condemn us, God is greater than our heart, and knoweth all things. Beloved, if our heart condemn us not, then have we confidence toward God.
1 John 3:20-21, KJV

The Holy Spirit deals with our conscience to transform us from the inside so we can have confidence toward God. Believe me, it will free us from the manipulation of the devil and we'll no longer feel driven or held captive by any condemnation of our conscience. Whenever we feel condemned, we lose confidence toward God. God is greater than our hearts or conscience and He knows our motives. Focus on Jesus and let the Holy Spirit remove condemnation and restore our confidence towards God. We can then remain "Son conscious," not "sin conscious," and sail effortlessly by the Wind of the Spirit.

*A new power is in operation. The **Spirit of life** in Christ, like a **strong wind**, has magnificently cleared the air, freeing you from a fated lifetime of brutal tyranny at the hands of **sin and death**.*
Rom. 8:2, MSG [emphasis mine]

Freedom

Jesus never imposes a yoke of law nor a heavy burden of religion on us. He says just the opposite: His yoke is easy, His burden is light [Matt.11:30]. He's not just saying that His burden isn't heavy. I believe He is saying, His burden is so light that it's like a helium balloon, *lifting us up*. It's anti-gravity. His yoke is so easy, that when we "yoke up" and flow with Him, we're like one of those tiny fish that attach themselves to a whale. We just cling to Him and He gets us to where we are going. That's how we find rest and freedom. He leads us in His plan, purposed specifically for us, satisfying and fulfilling all our hopes and dreams. It will surprise us of the plan He has for us. It is above and beyond anything we could have imagined!

When my focus was on self, I found myself *incarcerated* under the law, never able to enjoy the inheritance left to me. I needed to be set free of self. It's what we deal with when we are "law minded" and not "Grace minded."

> *...God sent his Son, born among us of a woman, born under the conditions of the law so that he might redeem those of us who have been **kidnapped by the law**. Thus we have been set free to experience our rightful **heritage**.*
>
> Gal. 4:4-5, MSG [emphasis mine]

However, listening to the "Good News Gospel" will change the way we live life. Then the focus on our own performance will fade away. Our minds will be renewed and a change in our life is guaranteed.

The Lord said to me, "True, unconditional love gives the freedom of choice." At first, choice may seem a bit scary because we are so aware that choices in the past may have put us in places we didn't want to be. However, there is peace when we realize that we're joint heirs and partners on this journey with Jesus. Even though we make choices, He is there to lead us and help us. Let's focus on Him and not on our past. That's when we will find that the choices are not as risky as we once perceived them.

First off, our choices never catch our Father off guard. He's omniscient and already knows our tomorrow. That gives us rest and freedom. He will show us when we're off course and on our own self-made "passion for performance plan." When He does, we can choose to "come about" [turn around]. Then watch, He will put His hands to the helm and get us back on course, in His plan.

Second, by relying on the Holy Spirit as our navigator, we will be amazed at how difficult He makes it for us to get off course. You see, His love *compels* and *woos* us to go on with Him and that's powerful. Once we've tasted of the freedom in Christ, we don't want to go back. Who wants to go back to the "Port of Bondage" with that yuck feeling in the pit of your stomach?

Paul, the "bastion of truth," warned the Galatians not to take their freedom for granted and go back to old ways of "doing." Just that little bit of *leaven* permeates the whole loaf of bread. Don't let leaven get you off course!

Jesus at the Helm

For freedom did Christ set us free: stand fast therefore, and be not entangled again in a yoke of bondage.

Gal. 5:1, ASV

This new liberty in Jesus has been misunderstood by many and under-enjoyed by more. Discovering this new freedom in the Grace Gospel can be a bit disconcerting at first. It can feel like you are stepping out on thin ice, wondering, "Is it real and will it hold me? Can this Gospel be that good?" This is actually when our trust in Him kicks in. We defined "trust" earlier as "a reliance or *resting* of the *mind* on the *integrity* and *friendship* of another person."

Is your relationship with Jesus based on a friendship? Do you see him as your Groom, to whom you are married? My wife is my best friend in the natural. Jesus wants to be our best friend, who we can trust with our whole life. That allows us to experience freedom and rest our minds in the integrity and faithfulness of His friendship. He is our Inheritance and our Portion.

*Because of the sacrifice of the Messiah, his blood poured out on the altar of the Cross, we're a free people – free of penalties and punishments chalked up by all our misdeeds. And **not just barely free**, either. **Abundantly free**.*

Eph. 1:7, MSG [emphasis mine]

Let's magnify Jesus and we will see God get bigger and circumstances shrink. Grace has brought us safe this far and Grace will take us home.

As I've said earlier in the book, the first three words I heard the Father speak to me were, "God is Fun!" I believe that's our ministry [my mate and I], and it's a *high calling*. Think about it, God has to remind us that He is a fun God! He wants us to have fun and enjoy life wherever we go. He wants us to sail our journey with *joy* that brings *endurance*. It happens by keeping our focus on Jesus.

Give Him all your worries and cares. Pull up anchor, check the wind, set your sails. We have destinations over the horizon. Steady as you go.

There's an **extraordinary voyage** ahead and an **inheritance** waiting to be discovered!

Jesus at the Helm

All sunshine and sovereign is God, generous in gifts and glory. He doesn't scrimp with his traveling companions. It's smooth sailing all the way with God of the Angel Armies.
Ps. 84:11-12, MSG

About the Author

It was at a Jesus Youth Center, in his twenties, that Jerry was miraculously delivered from a long-time addiction to alcohol and drugs. It was here that he began teaching and counseling. However, an underlying problem had crept into his life, worse than drugs and alcohol. He had let himself come under the unmerciful clinches of "Law and Religion" and within a few years he had fallen back into his former addictions, worse than before! After 19 years living this lifestyle and running from God, he finally came to the end of himself. While contemplating suicide, Jerry felt the Wind of God blowing again in his life. God had miraculously shifted His wind and all the currents of circumstances, to sail Jerry right into the "Port of Grace." It was from there that he began an all new, Spirit-filled journey with Jesus on the "Seas of Grace." It was a new and living way that he began sharing wherever he went.

In ministry, he spent a number of years as teacher, counselor, and singles pastor. He could be found teaching and preaching in meetings, churches and wherever invited, as well as heading up and facilitating numerous life groups and home cell groups. Jerry met his wife, Crystal, at Charis Bible College where they both

About the Author

graduated and were licensed. They were ordained through Safe Harbor International and began their Grace Journey together, openly sharing this Grace Gospel message. They have seen numerous lives changed and delivered from the captivity of "Law and Religion" and have seen many return to their "First Love." Their vision is to see people having a renewed relationship with Jesus and their Abba Father and to flow under the banner of the Grace Message that Paul had so radically taught.

www.ingramcontent.com/pod-product-compliance
Lightning Source LLC
Chambersburg PA
CBHW072344090426
42741CB00012B/2911